Nutrition and Religion

Nutrition and Religion

By

D. Usha Rani,
M. V. Sudhakara Reddy,
M. Sreedevamma

2003

DISCOVERY PUBLISHING HOUSE
NEW DELHI-110002

Published by:
Namit Wasan

DISCOVERY PUBLISHING HOUSE PVT. LTD.
4383/4B, Ansari Road, Darya Ganj
New Delhi-110 002 (India)
Phone : +91-11-23279245; 23253475; 43596065
E-mail : discoverybooksindia@gmail.com
discoverypublishinghouse@gmail.com
namitwasan9@gmail.com
web : www.discoverypublishinggroup.com

Edition: 2020

ISBN: 978-81-7141-648-6

Nutrition and Religion

Printed at:
Infinity Imaging Systems
Delhi

Preface

Life styles of people differ with different socio-economic, socio-cultural and religious backgrounds. Nutritional patterns are affected not only by socio-economic and socio-cultural backgrounds of communities but also by religion. Religions plays a significant role in the lives of Indians to the extent that it imposes several restrictions even on the foods consumed by them. This book on nutritional patterns among different religious communities is eye opening and reveals the effect of religious taboos on food consumption. The beliefs that people hold about foods to be consumed and avoided leaves much to be desired. The nutritional status and consequent health of the elderly, pregnant and lactating women, infant and childcare practices are being greatly affected by religious taboos on foods. The high rate of malnutrition in the Indian society is traced to the social customs and inimical cultural practices dictated by religion. Restrictions on foods as related to religious beliefs are prevalent to a large extent. As such better knowledge about nutrition, health and childcare practices is the need of the day. In this context, special education programmes need to be offered to combat malnutrition and unhealthy nutritional practices. This book is particularly useful for students, teachers and extensions workers engages in health care and developmental programmes.

D. Usha Rani,
M.V. Sudhakara Reddy,
M. Sreedevamma

Contents

1. Introduction

Nutritional practices play a significant role in maintaining the health status of an individual. Practices permitting an adequate diet (in quality and quantity) contribute to the health of the individual. An adequate diet has a marked effect upon a person's vitality, emotional stability and enthusiasm for life and work.

Nutritional practices or habits may be defined as "the way in which individuals or groups of individuals in response to social and cultural pressures, select, consume and utilize portions of the available food supply" *(Guthe and Mead, 1943)*. In other words the practices are determined by a person's choices, preferences and preparations and are influenced by a number of external factors such as beliefs, customs, traditions, prejudices and practices in a community.

Nutritional practices and patterns are developed by people's tendency to settle into fixed habits. Eventually, they characterize regional and national eating practices either poor or good. Poor food habits are seen in a person who eats only what he likes with total disregard to the quality of food and to the possibility that they may not add up to an adequate diet. These habits may also be due to poverty and other deprivations. Good food habits on the other hand are judged by the willingness and interest a person shows in eating the kinds and amounts of foods which are needed for nutritional adequacy. Thus the food habits of a community furnish presumptive evidence of the nutritional status of its population.

The nutritional status of an individual is the result of many interacting factors operating simultaneously on the individual in the physical, ecological and cultural setting of the community. Attempts to improve nutritional conditions cannot be made intelligently unless the factors other than the knowledge of nutrition which determine food choices are known and considered. The quantity of various foods purchased and consumed and the associated food practices or habits are a reflection of the economic conditions and the social, cultural and educational values of a community.

A proper appreciation of the economic, social and cultural factors conditioning the dietary habits of communities is essential for the implementation of any nutrition programme. Traditional aversions, prohibitions and beliefs frequently limit the range or choice of foods that might provide some additional nutrients. Therefore nutrition cannot be considered in isolation. The economic, social and cultural background of those whose nutritional patterns are to be improved should form the basis for any nutrition policy.

In order to overcome the vicious cycle of malnutrition, nutritionists need to be aware of the religious values, customs, beliefs, tradition bounded attitudes and practices which compose the total cultural pattern of any community. *Aykroyed (1961)* indicates that if one wants to improve the diet of any human group then one must know something about the existing food consumption pattern of the group because that is the starting point of improvement. But mere knowledge of what people eat is not enough. One must probe and gain understanding of why they eat, what they do—an understanding, that is of the numerous factors—economic, social, cultural, psychological and environmental which underline dietary practices. *Ranganathan (1968)* stresses that as far as possible one should try to respect the existing socio-cultural norms and beliefs with regard to food in a locality while efforts are made to improve the nutritional status.

The above information leads one to understand that many factors—economic, social, psychological, cultural—play a role in moulding the food consumption patterns of any given population.

Religion is one of the numerous factors influencing Nutritional practices. According to Webster's dictionary Religion is the service and adoration of God through worship in obedience to divine commands found in the scared writings and through the following of a way of life regarded as incumbent on true believers. *Brown (1955)* stated that every religion has provided ways by which man can try to relate to a supreme being or some supernatural force. Many of the practices and beliefs of the various religions of man are attempts to explain those things which man himself cannot understand or control. Each religion has evolved certain rituals or customs, the observance of which is believed to be very important since this reaffirms the various beliefs of the religion. The formal religions of the world have long and, a marked influence on the dietary habits of people of the world. Each major religion is different but each has very specific, strict rules and codes delineating what is acceptable as food *(Lowenberg et al, 1974).*

Food, man's most precious and sometimes scarce possession has become associated with many of the religious rituals. The practice of offering food or abstaining from food has provided man in his every day, life with a symbolic way to indicate his devotion, respect and love to his supreme being. Within each religion, the various symbolic ways of using food has had deep meaning to men. Religion thus, from hundreds of years has been having profound influence on man's dietary practices and habits with all its attendant taboos and prejudices. The study of food consumption patterns of populations belonging to different religions is important in this context, as action (to improve nutritional status) can be contemplated only on the basis of concrete knowledge regarding the nutritional practices of different sections of the populations.

Thus it can be stated that an assessment of food consumption patterns is essential to any investigation on the relationship between diet and health. Information about the dietary patterns of population can form the basis of programmes of agricultural production, food processing and food education and can indicate ways in which a nation's food supply might be made nutritionally adequate. Information about diets helps to identify undernourished and overnourished sections of the population, suggests ways in which diets might be improved and indicates the need for further clinical and epidemiological investigations.

Though attempts have been made to alter the patterns of food consumption in developing countries like India, they have been rather limited on account of paucity of information on the various factors and specially the cultural factors which influence food intake. Majority of the people are not used to thinking in terms of quality of food and they are also not aware of the need for special kinds of food for different ages. These aspects generally lead to malnutritional status.

Gopalan (1986) states that the majority of Indian children are still in a state of undernutrition as assessed by anthropometric measurements. Despite the green revolution and the significant contributions of nutritionists toward understanding the problem of malnutrition and offering solutions, the children continue to be undernourished in large sections of the rural and urban population.

Health statistics of India show that in the past twenty years, there has been little change in the pre-school children's mortality rate which has remained almost stationary. The high mortality rate in the pre-school children (17 as against 3 in Sri Lanka) is not occurring due to poor health and nutritional inadequacy alone but also due to the adverse influence of food fads, beliefs and prejudices over the choice of foods. Food preparations and menu planning are known to be subjected to seasonal variations not because of changes in the availability of foods alone but also because of certain beliefs attached to the effects of these food items in different seasons.

Considering all the above factors it is essential that the attitudes of the people about 'Food and health' be changed to establish good nutritional practices. In order to achieve this, it is important to study the various factors influencing Nutritional practices in different regions. It is of particular importance for countries like India where different religions and religious rituals abound where malnutrition has become an ever recurring phenomenon.

The present study was undertaken with the view that food is a prime necessity of life and that there are no other practices or habits which can influence the health of an individual as much as the decisions that are made with regard to bodily nourishments. It is essential therefore that decision making on this important aspect of life be properly guided and not conditioned by pseudo-scientific or faddists influences. The present investigator undertook to study various factors which may affect food choices of people, belonging to different religious communities in Tirupati. The existence of various religious groups in this pilgrim town and the fact that only limited research of this nature was done upto now in this area influenced the selection of this problem.

The study is an attempt to provide guidelines for improving the food selection patterns and through it the nutritional and health status of the people. The study may form the basis for nutrition education programmes designed to improve the nutritional status of different population groups.

The investigator studied the relation of various socio-economic factors (income, education, occupational levels) to the total food expenditure of the representative sample of the population in Tirupati. It also assessed the nutritional practices of vulnerable groups like pregnant and lactating mother and children.

Six hundred and fifty families were selected at random from different wards of Tirupati town. Information on various aspects of Nutritional practices were obtained by using a schedule.

The objectives of this investigation were:

1. to study the nutritional patterns among the selected sample of families belonging to different religious committees;
2. to study the factors—economic, social and cultural associated with the nutritional patterns of families belonging to different religious communities;
3. to describe and compare food beliefs and superstitions existing among families of different religious communities;
4. to find out whether religion affects the nutritional patterns with special reference to children, pregnant and lactating mothers;
5. to study a few aspects related to environment and health of the families among the different religious communities.

2. Review of Literature

Development is progress and advancement in all aspects of human life. Efforts to achieve better nourishment, health, education, living conditions, employment opportunities and leisure for the people of the world refers to 'Socio-economic development'. Therefore socio-economic development essentially involves a unified approach which reflects a consciousness of conceptual and empirical inter-relatedness of all aspects of human life *(U.N. Social Deve. Rev., 1970)*.

Of the various aspects of socio-economic development better nourishment directs attention to human nutrition. Human nutrition is the outcome of the sum total of the influences exerted by numerous activities, thoughts, sentiments and beliefs on the food practices of a group or community. Food is thus intimately woven into the life fabric of the society. The family and through it the individual, derive their food habits from the society of which they are integral parts. The cultural and social values, the economic conditions and the educational levels of a community are reflected in the food practices and habits of its people *(Sai, 1966)*.

Thus food is the final outcome of many interacting factors operating simultaneously and concurrently on the individual in the physical, ecological and cultural setting of the community. The amount of various foods and nutrients consumed by different segments of the population depend on food production, availability, logistics of distribution, economic systems, cultural milieu, educational levels and food habits of the people. The food practices (or) habits in turn reflect the cultural, social and educational values and the economic conditions of a community.

What people eat depends on many factors, including the availability of food. Food is not only something to eat and satisfy hunger, but also the symbol of social status, prosperity or poverty and the focus of emotional associations of love and hate, pleasure and pain, and satisfactions and disappointments. Man is a social being. He is born into a culture. His early childhood experiences are conditioned by the customs, traditions and modes of his society. They socialize his natural functions from birth, consequently, biological hunger is transformed into culturally determined appetite and socially patterned practices governed by economic factor. Therefore, nutrition cannot be considered in isolation.

Nutrition is thus closely related to several aspects of human life. An understanding of these factors are thereafter imperative.

The various macro level variables which Affect Nutritional practices can be categorised as follows:

Macro Level Variables

Economic Factor

Cultural Factor

Beliefs, Superstitions, Taboos, Attitudes and Practices

Customs and Traditions

Child Rearing Practices

Joint Family System

Religion

Social Factor

Ecological Factor

Availability of Food

Geographical Location

Floods, Famines and Wars

Industrialisation and Urbanisation

Psychological Factors

Other Factors

Education

Knowledge in Nutrition

Population

Embracing all these factors is the influence of women, who are the decision makers in the home.

Economic Factors

Economic status has a definite bearing on the amount of food people eat for it is income that decides the standard of living of a family. The poor generally spend a high proportion of their income on food (in South India the poorest families spend 80 per cent of their budgets on food, the affluent only 45 per cent). More money generally means a better diet. As the poor enjoy some increase in income, they devote a big fraction of that increase to additional food expenditures. In rural India when the very poor have extra income to spend, 75 per cent of its goes for food. This percentage declines as total income increases. The upper income rural Indians spend only 34 per cent of each additional increase of income on food.

Income levels also set the pattern of foods to be purchased and consumed. The poor spend most of it on food-grains, the rich much less so. The allocation for careals declines and that for milk products increases as households move into the middle class income levels. Also higher the income, larger is the percentage of the increase spent on fruits, vegetables and other variety food items.

Thus, income is a major determinant of diet quantity and quality. The traditional relationship between the amount of family income and the pattern of food expenditure was discovered by the German Civil Servant Engle (1857). It has become known as Engles law. The law states that "As income increases, smaller is the relative percentage of the total outlay spent for food". In Western countries, Engle's law of food expenditure has been amply verified. The evidence shows:

(1) Until the starvation level is passed, additional increments of income are associated for a period at least, with increased proportion spent for food.

(2) Additional increases in income are associated with an increasing amount spent for food, but at a rate which leads to a decreasing proportion of the total income. These relations occur among populations securing food sufficient for existence and comfort.

(3) Finally as income increases further there is some evidence that the amount spent for food may actually decrease. The upper sedentary and rich classes are in this category.

A similar study by *Burgess and Dean (1962)* shows that the levels of living depend ultimately on levels of income. In the lower income groups, whose expenditure on food may exceed 50 per cent of the total income, any rise in economic status is usually reflected in an increase in the quantity of food consumed with little change in quality. At higher economic levels, however increased income usually results in greater expenditure on foods much as meat, eggs, and milk products with a consequent improvement in the nutritive value of family diets. At yet higher levels, expenditure on foods may increase further, but this may not result in an improvement in the diet from the nutritional stand point. Well-to-do families tend to prefer expensive cuts of meat, packaged foods, fruits out of season, and other luxuries, such as butter fat, candies, cakes and ice cream which may prove detrimental to health.

The Department of Employment and Productivity of England (1971) conducted a survey of food expenditure in Great Britain and Northern Ireland. Expenditure on different items of housing, fuel, food, clothing, household and other goods, transport and services was tabulated for households of 12 income groups. Total weekly expenditure ranged from £ 173.99 for households with income under £ 6 to £ 157.91 with £ 6 to £ 8 income. On an average the food cost, 86 per cent of total expenditure.

Florencio (1969) studied certain working class families in Columbia, for their efficiency of food expenditure their nutrition and how expensively they could have done so. Linear programming was used to know the least-cost diets that would meet the levels of nutritional allowances. The average columbian family in the sample spent 59 per cent of food for buying nutrients and 41 per cent for other objectives. The most efficient family spent 77 per cent of its actual food expenditure for nutrition, while the least efficient family spent only 37 per cent.

In a more recent survey *Hausen (1973)* has shown that among the American families only 16 per cent of the income is spent for food as compared to 25 to 40 per cent in Western Europe and 75 to 90 per cent in developing countries. The poor income groups tend to eat more breads and cereals while the middle and high income groups consume more meat, poultry, fish, milk and milk products, fruits and vegetables.

Mckenzie (1974) noted the impact of economic choice on food choice. There is an abundance of evidence from both developed and developing countries to demonstrate that the richer people have a more adequate, varied and palatable diet. There is a steady decline in the consumption of milk, meat and fruit as one goes down in social classes with growth in consumption of bread and potatoes. On a world wide basis, a similar picture emerges, if one looks at the percentages of total energy intake derived from cereals, starch roots and sugar. Thus 80 per cent of the energy is derived in this way in the far Eastern region, 72 per cent in the near East and 74 per cent in Africa compared to 63 per cent in Europe, 48 per cent in Oceania and 40 per cent in North America.

Poleman (1973) explains the effect of income on food habits of Sri Lanka. Among the poor, whether for the country as a whole or for individuals, the diets are characteristically dominated by the starchy staple foods, the cereals and starchy fruits, roots and tubers. This is because for their relative cheapness, whether expressed in terms of market price or production costs. The under Rs. 200/- income groups were thus lacking in quality diets, calories, proteins, vitamins and minerals were deficient in these diets.

Devadas and Easwaran (1971) noted that the economically better off consume a variety side dishes and found that the percentages of food consumption and expenditure on protective foods like meat, eggs and fish increases with increases in income whereas the intake of cereal decreases.

Rao (1967) also found through his dietary surveys that although people had upward trends in the consumption of protective foods, low income and inadequate supply of protective foods appeared to have left the diet almost static over this decade. With such inadequacies and no special foods given to supplement the diet of children or pregnant women, malnutrition is rampant.

Thimmayamma, Satyanarayana, Swaminathan, Parvathi (1973) undertook a family diet survey among the different income groups I–Superintendent; Group II–clearks, and group III–Attenders in the Hyderabad city. The result showed that the diet and nutrient intake was almost adequate except for few nutrients in group I and II The quality of the diet in the income group III was observed to be poor resulting in the deficiency of almost all the nutrients except calcium. Expenditure pattern on food showed that 82 per cent of the total income was spent on food in the income group III while 40 and 43 per cent of the total income was spent on food in the groups I and II respectively. There were no major differences in the expenditure pattern on various food groups between the groups I and II. The striking feature in the expenditure on food in group III was that 43 per cent of the total expenditure incurred on food was on flesh foods. The amount eaten per C.u/day however, was very small. The expenditure on sugar and jaggery and oils was also low in the group III. The above findings suggest that an increase in the income level has a definite impact on the quality and quantity of the diet of the families. There was a greater variety in the diets of the families belonging to group I and II as compared to group III and also higher intake of milk and pulses. Mention may be made here that families in group I and II belonged to a certain socio-economic strata and their food habits were some what fixed by their way of living.

Devadas et. al., (1967) also found that income appeared to have a decisive influence in that the low income group had a predominantly cereal diet from the post-weaning stage, while the middle income families included cereals, pulses, vegetables and negligible amounts of protective food like milk and flesh foods in the diets for their children. The upper income families had more balanced diets for their children with cereals and protective foods, although leafy vegetables did not find a place in their menus. The clinical assessment of the children also showed that the nutritional status of the upper income group children was better than the middle and low income groups, the latter showing the poorest picture.

Another study by *Rao (1978)* among urban and rural groups reported that purchasing power is obviously a major determinant of food intake. It was observed that cereals appear much more in rural consumption than in urban consumption at all expenditure levels while the reverse is the case with beverages and refreshments. Milk and milk products figure more in urban consumption except that the difference declines as one moves up to the higher expenditure classes. Meat, fish and egg figure more in urban consumption except for the three lowest expenditure classes. The combined item of fruits and vegetables figure much more in the urban areas in all expenditure classes, fruits accounting for a higher degree of differences than vegetables. Edible oils figure more in urban consumption at all expenditure levels while sugar figures more in urban consumption at all expenditure levels except the three highest categories where it figures more in rural consumption.

To sum up an overview of the studies on economic status highlight the impact of income on food expenditure pattern. The studies indicate that at low levels of income an increase in economic status generally results in increasing the quantity of food consumed with little or on change in quality. At higher income levels an increasing economic status results in raising the quality of foods consumed consequently improving the nutritive value of family diets. However, at still higher levels of income, a further increase in income may not necessarily result in an improvement in the diet from the nutritional stand point. Rather the choice may be more towards expensive processed foods which may prove detrimental to health.

It is seen from the above studies that nutritional status has a definite bearing on the food people etc. While it is true that increased income levels beneficially affect the nutritional status of households, yet it is also true that income rises very slowly for the poor and even that increased purchasing power often cannot overcome certain food habits and practices that stand in the way of effective nutritional improvement, especially in the cases of young children, pregnant women and lactating mothers. Increased income is not a sufficient condition for adequate nutrition. Explicit steps such as the establishment of special food distribution, mechanisms and supportive measures in education will be required to reinforce the dietary benefits from higher income. It these supportive measures are to be successful, it is necessary to find out the influence of various other factors on Nutritional practices of the people of which cultural factors are very important.

Cultural Factors

Nutritional practices are always defined culturally, what, how, when and where one eats are largely determined by one's culture.

Fathaver (1960) says that 'Food' is always defined culturally and the same plant may be defined as edible by one society and inedible by another.

Every culture has its own strong preferences for certain kinds of foods and cooking at certain timings and sequences of meals eaten are according to a local ritual with knives and forks, chopsticks or with fingers on plates or banana leaves as the case may be *(Aykroyd, 1961)*. It is also pointed out that cultural preferences stem from an interplay between food supplies, tradition and the necessities imposed by the material and social environment.

Mortagn and Lee have pointed out that what, how, when and where one eats is largely determined by one's culture *(Mortagn, 1957; Lee, 1957)*.

Proudfit and Robinson (1965) say that the meal patterns themselves are dictated by culture. They reported that for many Americans breakfast is a hearty meal which can be well rationalized on the basis of physiological need; the European, however, is more accustomed to a light breakfast—perhaps bread or a roll without butter, and coffee—and finds it difficult to consume a meal as he considers it to be heavy. The farmer may prefer to have dinner at noon, while the urban worker away from home all day, has his biggest meal in the evening.

Guthe and Mead (1943) indicate that in each generation, children learn the traditional food habits of their families and these habits in turn are passed on to their children.

Parvathi Rao (1968) indicates that the cultural attitudes, values, practices and beliefs regarding the intake of food among the different groups in a community are meaningful and are of great importance to nutrition.

Fleck and Munves (1962) say that a culture defines the foods which are edible or inedible. People may have strong guilt feelings about eating a food considered inedible by their group. They referred that long ago a Frenchman, M. Serrel pointed out that there are over two million species of animals and only 50 species are domesticated and eaten. Of the 25,000 known species of vegetables only about 600 are cultivated.

Cassel (1957) indicated that in Zulu tribesmen, one of the major factors influencing the inadequacy of the diet is certain traditions which decide as to which foods should be eaten.

Foster (1962) in his book "Traditional Cultures and The Impact of Technological Change" reported, that culture is the strong barrier in changing the food habits. He cited the following example:

In India, a village worker asked a farmer about his reaction to a new wheat that had been tried experimentally for several years. The villager replied that it was better in appearance, brought a higher price and was more resistant to rain and frost. Then he added "but the local variety is better in taste" and concluded "from the point of view of health there is nothing like it" *(Foster, 1962)*.

Byrne et. al., (1962) indicated that of major importance in the whole cultural background of the family are the Beliefs Superstitions, Taboos, Attitudes and Practices about food.

Beliefs, Superstitions, Taboos, Attitudes and Practices

These factors concerning food are powerful and can pose problems in nutrition education. Family attitudes regarding health and disease influence the attitudes regarding feeding the members. Women and children are often the direct victims of discriminations in food priorities. Prevailing customs may prevent people from consuming valuable foods, even when they are available. In the traditional Indian society men and children eat first and women last. Men receive a larger quantity of food than women.

Beliefs are crucial in the acceptance or rejection of foods. The beliefs of any community are the products of social interactions deeply entrenched in the minds of that community because of deep faith. Many of the food fads and fallacies stem from ignorance about nutritive values of foods and quantitative and qualitative requirements. Wrong beliefs and practices are the results of such ignorance.

Family attitudes towards the feeding of children and pregnant women in health and disease are often the direct causes of malnutrition. Prevailing belief may prevent people from consuming a valuable foods even when available. Some foods like rice in South India, have stigma attached to them. Feeding habits are so inter-twined with the culture and value systems that changes in one area are bound to be influenced or occasioned by changes in the other.

Dhillon reported that cheap, available foods rich in provitamin A; such as pappaya and green leaves are often with held from young children because they considered to produce cold. These type of ideas can have serious consequences in a country, such as Malaysia, where eye diseases caused by a deficiency of 'Vitamin A' are prevalent.

Cultural considerations control the diet in lactation. The new mother is not allowed to eat any new food, as it is believed to affect the health of the child when she is feeding. But, she is given extra milk, ghee, garlic rasam, jaggery water and white gourd (ash gourd) for increasing her milk. Brinjal, drumstick leaves and roasted bengal gram are avoided as they would 'dry up' the milk in the breast. Biscuits are the food commonly given to children as supplements at weaning, in the belief, that they are good for health and digestible.

During puberty, the foods given are enormous quantities of rice, gingelly seeds, eggs (for non-vegetarians) and milk, These are to build up the stamina of the young girls for meeting the nutritional and physiological challenges and stresses of motherhood in the future.

Leverton (1960) says that there is a kind of food misinformation which can be dangerous tool. These are myths and superstitions which have been woven around food and handed down from one generation to another. Some people believe the old wives tales about the good and bad qualities of different foods. Some of these beliefs are listed as follows:

1. Milk is a food only for children and grown ups do not need it;
2. Milk eaten with fish or with sour fruits in harmful;
3. Meat is hard on the kidneys;
4. Fruits juices cause an acid condition in the body;
5. Apple ceder vinegar makes the body to burn fat instead of storing it.

Whiteman (1961) reported about food habits of people in Nigeria. Oranges, grapes fruit, pappaya and mangoes grow well in Nigeria but many will not eat them as they are associated with feminity by some and with intestinal worms by others.

Jenner (1968) reported that fresh fruits grew in abundance in West China but little use was made of them, with the exception of citrus fruits. The reason given was that fresh fruits make people sick.

All cultures have certain beliefs related to food such as 'hot' or 'cold' and 'light' or 'heavy' without any scientific basis. *Jenner (1968), Parvathi Rao (1968)* and *Rajammal Devadas (1968)* reported that the concept of hot or cold is not in terms of the temperature sense, but in the sense that some foods are believed to produce heat in the body and therefore deemed suitable for certain conditions like cold and stomach pain. Similarly cold foods produce a cooling effect and therefore good for conditions such as fever which require cooling. Based on such beliefs, children suffering from infectious diseases are given only fluid diets for long periods of time. Some cultural groups refuse to give fish to children since fish is believed to produce worms.

Thus many prohibitions and taboos affect the consumption of valuable food by expectant and nursing mothers and children. *Aykroyd (1961)* reported that some African people think that eggs, meat and fish have bad effects on the health of children and mothers.

A monthly magazine *"Freedom from Hunger" (1967)* gives some examples of food prejudices. The are as follows: In some communities new mothers are made to consume a diet of rice and salt for a prolonged period, just when the mother needs protein rich foods to allow her to breast feed successfully. In some remote villages of developing countries the people believe a person will grow to look like the source of food he consumes and for this reason will not drink goat's milk. In parts of Latin America, babies are fed grapes because the mother believes they will thus learn to talk at an earlier age. In some African villages, eggs are forbidden food for women and children—for women, because they are believed to cause sterility end for children probably to discourage theft of eggs from sitting hens.

Edwards et. al., (1954) reported the influence of superstitions on food habits of women. In Manning, South Carolina, there is a traditional belief that milk, eggs, fish yellow vegetables, grape fruit, tomatoes, butter, liver and beans should not be eaten. In Anniston, Alabama, the belief also extends to other foods, such as bacon, yam and onions. The eating of green food appears to be a taboo during the post partum period among women in Lovisiana. Approximately one third of the women who visit the country health department, reported that they eat only rice, potatoes and milk during the postpartum period. This may be due to the idea that green colour of vegetables might show up in the mother's milk. Fish, too is widely tabooed in North Carolina, Georgia, South Carolina and Kentucky. As many as 35 per cent of the rural Negro women apparently adhere to this practice. Comments indicated that some felt it would poison them and others stated that it would prove fatal if consumed for several weeks after child birth. The continuation of "fish and milk" was thought to be specially dangerous. Other strange, ill found notions included that cheese, bananas and ice cream will make a person sick, cooked cabbage and other "strong-tasting" greens will upset the stomach and 'taint' the milk.

Moller (1961) reported that there are two general food taboos for adult women of Waluguen in Tanganyika. They are not allowed to eat eggs or twin bananas as they are supposed to lead to the risk of having twins, which is a serious misfortune. Other beliefs of consumption of eggs by women are that they may lead to irregular menstruation or disappearance of it altogether and that if a woman becomes pregnant, the child will be still born.

Devadas (1968) reported that in some South Indian villages, no special food is given to pregnant women, but the quantity of rice and milk are restricted for fear of the foetus becoming 'big' and making the delivery difficult. Similarly the new lactating mother should not eat any new food, as it will affect the health of the child when she is feeding. But she is given extra milk, ghee, garlic rasam, jaggery water and ash gourd for increasing her milk. Brinjal, drumstick leaves and roasted bengal gram are avoided as they would 'dry up' the milk in the breast.

Rajyalakshmi (1969) reported some of the beliefs existing in India. Pappaya is believed to cause abortions. Jaggery is believed to heat up the body system. In South India, wheat is believed to be heat giving and to be harmful. Bananas are believed to result in convulsions in children and even death. Potatoes, pumpkin etc., are believed to result in Flatus (gas) particularly in children and nursing mothers. Butter milk is believed to result in sore throat and is avoided by persons having cold. Peepper is believed to stimulate blood formation. It is also believed that a diet lacking in spices is not easily digested. Ghee is believed to have strength giving properties and is more easily digested than groundnut oil or other oils.

Williams (1973) states that some customs, beliefs and tradition have a good influence on dietary practices of the people. The report reveals that the birth of a child is observed in many cultures by a meal that symbolizes a general celebration of the beginning of life. It is an occasion for fasting or in some cultures for offering special foods to one or more deities. Soon after birth, a baptism or dedication ceremony may be followed by a special family feed. Birthdays are celebrated with special foods in modern America, with a cake decorated with candles. Weddings are especially surrounded with symbolic foods. The bride's cake and the wedding reception are common in western culture.

Maliha and Umapathi (1976) in their report stated that food habits and food beliefs are among the oldest and most entranched aspects of any culture. They are influenced by customs, social pattern and most of other factors. Five hundred mothers belonging to different income groups who were admitted for participation in five hospitals and clinics of Mysore city were interviewed with an oral questionnaire. The information regarding personal and family background; usual food consumption pattern; foods specially avoided or consumed during pregnancy and lactation; as well as pica habit during pregnancy were elicited. The food items which are said to be specially consumed during this period are pepper, betel leaves, garlic, mutton, milk, dry coconut and pawn. In general, the avoidance or special consumption of foods were centered around 'hot' and 'cold' concept of foods. Since a well established physiological basis for the concept is lacking, it is emphasized that more work needs to be done in this direction. Also, the possible beneficial or harmful effects of foods avoided or specially included during pregnancy and lactation from the nutritional and health points of view should be studied. The incidence of pica habit during pregnancy was found to be 18 per cent. Geophazia was found to be the most common form of pica. This habit was observed to decrease with an increase in the income and educational level of the couple. There is a need to investigate the causative factors of pica and possible implications on nutritional status in Indian society. It is also necessary to enlighten mothers of different income groups about the importance of including foods of high nutritional quality during pregnancy and lactation.

Customs and Traditions

Each family develops its own traditions in serving foods and any deviations from them can be distorting. Customs of cooking and handling food differ widely and social organisation of the domestic groups varies in different societies.

From one place to another opinions differ about certain foods; the belief that a particular food is dangerous, probably rests on mixture of traditional beliefs and personal experience.

Copping (1968) cited an example that in many African countries, it is rare to find men eating in a family group with wives and children. The cooking and distribution of food and the methods of serving and eating are traditional in any society and are taught to children in proverbs and stories.

Jenner (1968) reported that in certain parts of West Africa, the man of the family eats first, than come the sons, then the daughters and then the wife or wives. The man takes care to leave a little on his plate for the sons, to this the mothers may add a little but often she does not. The mother serves for herself in another dish what she and the daughter will eat, but the mother gives each daughter a piece of meat corresponding to about half of what she eats herself or to a fourth or fifth of what the father eats.

Devadas (1968) cited some of the customs of eating patterns existing in India. These are: the head of the family eats first then all the other sons, daughters and finally the wife and mother. The father-in-law gets and precedence over the husband. All the good items in the menu (ghee, curd) which are also likely to be limited in quantity are given first to men and children. Such order at meals affects the availability of meals to the other members specially to the mothers and children.

Jean (1950) found from his studies that women's food habits have been greatly influenced by marriage. Meals were planned according to the husband's likes and dislikes, superimposed on the wife's original dietary habits. If there were children, they also altered the mother's food habits.

These preceding studies show that customs, beliefs and superstitions are forceful in the use of foods. Many of the practices which stem from culture are harmful to nutrition since they are based on false notions and ignorance. *Gopalan (1966)* stresses that this cultural significance of foods plays a fundamental role in the struggle for existence. The studies reveal that every culture has its own preferences for various foods, cooking patterns, timing and sequence of meals.

Child Rearing Practices

Child rearing is not a technical term with precise significance. It is a continuous process and refers generally to all the interactions between parents and their children. These interactions include the parents' expression of attitudes, values interests and beliefs as well as their caretaking and training behaviour. *Seers et. al., (1957)* studied the influences of various factors like culture, socio-economic status, sex of the child and the ordinal position of the child on child rearing practices. He found that all these had varying influence on the child rearing practices.

McKenzie (1971) states that most of the infantile malnutrition in Uganda is due to the family weaning practices, tribal customs, taboos and broken homes. Moreover the indigenous populations have less appreciation and demand for milk and milk preparations for children.

Sharma, Siddhu and Prasad (1972) studied 234 children under 5 years belonging to 166 families of heterogeneus socio-economic status registered at urban health centre, Alanberg, from Sep. 1967 to Jan. 1969. A high percentage of infants were assured of sufficient quantity of milk upto 6 months and thereafter the lactating capacity of mothers declined progressively and by 18 months it was found to be grossly inadequate and yet breast feeding was continued without any substantial addition of solids or semisolids in a large proportion of cases. 'Demand' feeding was practised in 95.16 per cent of cases. In 92.8 per cent of mothers the standard of breast hygiene and cleanliness was poor. Sixty three per cent of children were weaned after the age of one year and 37 per cent between 18 and 30 months. Forty one per cent of children remained without additional calorific food (other then breast milk) even beyond the age of 18 months. Irregularity, insufficient quantity and undue dilution in the supplementary feeds were practised in majority of cases. Solid diet was introduced in 69 per cent after the age of one year. Dietary survey covering 210 children revealed protein and caloric inadequacy in over two-third and iron, calcium, Vit. A and riboflavin deficiencies in the diet in about half of the cases of study. Thirty one per cent of total children were clinically suffering from one or more deficiency conditions while half the investigated children were found to be anaemic.

Divekar (1967) undertook a project to study the child rearing practices among Marathi middle class families in Bombay. She reported that all the mothers pointed out changes in child rearing practices of the present as compared to those of the past. She then compared her findings with those of *Charulatha Seth (1967)* who studied the child rearing practices among the middle class Gujarati families. She found that though the two groups of mothers were from a similar income levels the child rearing practices varied in features like toilet training, eating practices, between the groups.

Ghosh, Gidwani, Mittal and Verma (1976) studied the infant feeding practices among 802 mothers as a part of a longitudinal study of birth cohort. Although all women practised breast feeding, 22.8 per cent stopped breast feeding before 6 months of age. Literate mothers tended to curtail breast feeding earlier than the illiterate mothers. Surprisingly younger women were found to breast feed the babies for a longer period than the older ones. Sex of the infant and the duration of the urban stay of the mothers did not seem to affect the duration of breast feed. Supplementation with animal milk was early and 50 per cent of the mothers diluted buffallo's milk. This milk was the most common animal milk used. Addition of semisolid and solid food was delayed, more so by the illiterate mothers.

Wadhwer and Wagle (1974) surveyed 200 families from poorer sections of the society with a total income of less than 350 rupees per month and residing in slums of Bombay. The study revealed the usual practices of prolonged breast feeding, delay in introducing solids beyond one year of age and rice and wheat + dhal as the staple foods of infants.

Jaiswal, Malik, Ansari, Sinha (1981) undertook a field-based longitudinal study to see the feeding practices and morbidity pattern during the first year of life in 57 per cent Muslim, 39 per cent Hindu and 4 per cent Christian mothers of different socio-economic groups and educational status. Of the total population only 37 per cent of mothers gave pre-lacteal feeds and colostrum was given by 17.2 per cent while honey was offered by 39 per cent and 24.1 per cent of mothers. Although all mothers breast fed their sibling initially, it was discontinued before 6 months by 53.8 per cent of educated mothers as compared to 70.3 per cent of illiterate women who continued till the end of the year. Significantly, 25 per cent of babies received tea as substitute to breast milk and 93.3 per cent of mothers, both educated and illiterate, were giving diluted top milk. Semi-solids and solids were introduced in only 29 per cent of babies while 18 per cent of them were getting iron and vitamin supplements.

Feeding habits of infants and children have been studied by *Ghosh (1966)* amongst six hundred mothers from South India. The study revealed that most of the mothers started breast feeding from the third day onwards; most of the babies were breast fed upto two years of life. Solid foods were introduced mostly at the age group of 1 to 1½ years. Neither the age of the mother nor the parity seem to influence the breast-feeding habits of the mother.

Data for ten anthropometric variables had been collected on a cross-sectional sample of 54 male infants varying in age from 3 to 15 months by *Sindhu, Grewal and Bhatnagar (1981)*. Twenty nine infants were completely dependent on breast milk. All the anthropometric parameters studied indicated that breast fed infants were better in physical growth upto 7 months of age as compared to the bottle fed infants of the same age group. After that, bottle-fed infants showed better physical growth than breast-fed infants. It is recommended that among breast-fed children weaning should not be delayed beyond 7th month.

Mehata, Pawan and Betkerur (1972) studied the feeding habits in 400 infants at the paediatric out patient ward of civil hospital. The study revealed that 91 per cent mothers had given prelacteal feed, and 98 per cent had initiated breast feeding. Breast milk was considered a balanced diet upto 6 months. The incidence of nutritional disorders increased with the age. Prolonged breast feeding, faulty and poor knowledge of infant diet and delayed weaning were major causes of nutritional disorders.

Ramathulasi (1968) studied child rearing practices in relation to factors like socio-economic status, ordinal position of the child, type of the family, age of the mother and sex of the child. She found that sex had the least influence on the child rearing practices.

Indira Bai (1970) in her article on infant feeding practices in South India with special reference to Tirupati quoted that the breast fed do not suffer from frequent infections as the bottle fed infants. Among the majority of the poorer population, semi-solid foods do not appear until late in the 1st year of life (9-12 months). No special food is prepared but children are given the more masticable food of the adult diet. Quite frequently these foods appear to be extremely indigestible, faulty and spiced. Egg and fish are not given with the belief that they produce cold. As a result the main deficiency states seen in these children are anaemias, avitaminosis A; marasmus, kwashiorkor and riboflavin deficiency. These feeding practices have an interplay with infection and malnutrition.

Feeding habits and child rearing customs were analysed by *Puri et. al., (1976)* in their study conducted in South India. Sugar in water was found to be a common initial pre-lacteal feed in the majority of infants. Breast feeding was delayed beyond 48 hours in most of the infants. The incidence of breast feeding was the commonest pattern of infant feeding. It was observed that the duration of breast feeding bore a definite inverse relationship to the education of the mother and economic status of the parents. Idly was the commonest initial solid food. An attempt was made to find out the various child rearing practices and food fads in this part of the country. It is postulated that food fads and an erroneous knowledge of the nutritive values of various diets are the main causes of high infant mortality and morbidity in South India. The community at large needs proper and correct health and nutrition education which is lacking in the present day health programme.

The sum up child rearing is a continuous process and generally refers to all the interactions between parents and their children. The above cited studies reveal that various factors like factors like culture, socio-economic status, sex of the child affect rearing practices. The studies have attempted to find out various child rearing practices and food fads in different parts of the country. They reveal that an erroneous knowledge of the nutritive values of various diets is the main cause of infant mortality and morbidity in India. The need of the day is proper and correct health and nutrition education which may improve the health trends in due course. Keeping this fact in view, a part of the present investigation was directed to secure information on the various child rearing practices among different religious groups.

Joint Family System

The joint family system is an important social institution. It is the cradle of customs and tradition and the nursery of culture. Most of the food habits are formed within that joint family in the early period of childhood.

Wilson and Widdowson (1933) reported that since both Hindus and Muslims tend to live in joint family groups, the number of inmates in any one household may be large and constantly fluctuating. It is well known characteristic of poor Indian families to cook the same amount of food, not matter how many persons are there to eat it. Thus the total amount of food eaten by the household is more constant than the amount available for each individual.

Monica Burne et. al., (1962) and Parvathi Rao (1968) indicated that in joint families, in the matter of child feeding and the diets of pregnant and lactating women, the mothers, mothers-in-law and grand mothers often have authority and this tells upon the nutrition of the vulnerable groups of population. A young mother, particularly one who needs help in the house with her children, does not like to antagonise the older women for fear of disapproval which thus forms into habits directed by the older women.

Thus even the type of a family to which a person belongs influence his nutritional practices. Therefore, of the many factors which affect the food habits of people, influence of the family system also should be studied in detail.

Religion

The rules of life laid down by each of the various religions in India include instructions as to dietary habits. Religion has played an important role in determining the food habits of the people and has to some extent influenced the general health of its followers for the better or for worse. Among the major religions of mankind, Buddhism preached effectively against the custom of eating animal food. Buddha's influence successfully prohibited the taking of life, for pleasure or eating. One of the most powerful kings of the ancient times, king Ashoka led a crusade against harming animals by humans. Under the influence of Buddhist thought a large number of people all over Asia are traditionally vegetarians and refuse to take any animal food except milk under any circumstances and are happy living on heavily starchy food.

Wilson and Widdowson (1933) reported some of the generally observed religious customs in the Indian community. Higher caste Hindus usually abstain from flesh but numerically the proportion of strict vegetarians among the Hindu population is small. Even the highest caste, Brahmins are in some remote areas considered above ordinary caste rule, and eat fowl and eggs. They also reported, that the Muslims do not observe caste. They are allowed to eat may meat except pork. The annual month of fast prescribed by the religion is generally observed, and families tend to increase their expenditure on food during this month, since more appetising food is considered necessary for meals taken at unaccustomed hours.

Ritchie (1967) reported that Mohammedans do not eat pork, most Hindus will not eat beef and some Hindu communities consume no food of animal origin except milk and milk products because their religion forbids the taking of life. The Jewish religion forbids pork, shell fish and the consumption of meat and dairy products at the same meal.

Proudfit and Robinson (1965) also reported that certain foods are forbidden by religious regulation. Pork is forbidden to the Orthodox Jews and to the Islamites. Buddhists are vegetarians. They eat no flesh of any animal, and many of them also refrain from eating eggs and milk.

Ritchie (1967) indicated that through many generations of observance while on the one hand religious restrictions have eliminated certain foods from the diet of some people, on the other hand religious feasts make an important contribution to normally poor diets in many regions of the world. He reported that Chinese, even when very poor, eat eggs and pork on the traditional festivals of the year, during special ceremonies, on the occasion of birth, death and other ceremonies, Poor Greek families eat lamb at Easter and on Sundays whenever possible, and this is sometimes the only meat they obtain.

Religious festivals are occasions for celebrations. *Devadas (1968)* reported from the surveys conducted in some Indian villages that the women, on these occasions, exhibit their dexterity in cooking. Even the poorest of the rural people prepare Vadai, Panchai Mavu (Raw rice flour ground and roasted), Kachayam (rice flour mixed in jaggery syrup and fried in deep fat either in small balls or flattened), Payasam, Laddu, Pongal and Biriyani on the festival occasions in the year. Some of the reasons given for the variety of foods prepared are:

to offer to God in thanks giving;

to pray to God for happiness in the future;

to have their secret desires fulfilled;

to eat well at least on a few days; and

to follow their customs and traditions.

Devadas (1968) also reported that children look forward to the festival days with great appetite. There are religious ceremonies, fasts and feasts with appropriate seasonal food preparations. For example, Vinayaka Chathurthi is celebrated with varieties of tasty and nutritional foods. Pongal is celebrated with cooking of new rice with sugarcane and Deepavali and Christmas are known for the varieties of sweet and savoury dishes. Onam festival in Kerala is famous for 22 varieties of preparations with root vegetables such as yam, tapioca, sweet potato and banana stem. On Fridays, which are auspicious for prayer the Hindus offer cooked rice and redgram dhal to God and the Christians abstain from eating meat, because on that day Jesus Christ was crucified. During "Ekadasi" in Maharashtra, Mysore, Andhra Pradesh, Tamil Nadu and other parts, sprouted grams are offered to God in prayers and distributed as snacks to children. During that season, all over West Bengal, Orissa and Assam, Durga Pooja is observed with hundreds of sweet preparations.

Apart from religion, the caste system puts several restrictions on feeding and some of the rules which are laid down by caste are:

the kinds of food a man may eat or abstain from eating;

the persons who may cook the food;

the rituals to be followed at meals;

the persons with whom one may take food and the nature; of the utensils that one may use for eating, drinking and cooking.

Many of the upper class castes follow these to preserve their purity *(Devadas, 1968)*.

Fleck and Munves (1962) pointed out that for centuries the religion of an individual has had a bearing on the way he feels about food. In most American homes there are still vestiges of feasts and first days and kinds of foods which are encouraged or forbidden by religious regulation about food. He may feel very virtuous of, he follows them and if he ignores them, he may have a serious feeling of guilt.

Thus various religions have prescribed certain food practices. The dietary restrictions imposed by religion determine the food habits of people. Some codes are helpful in promoting better nutrition, while others lead to malnutrition. The preceding studies indicate that various religions have laid down instructions as to the dietary habits its members should stick to over the generations. Observance of the religious restrictions have eliminated certain foods from the consumption pattern of the followers while some other rules regarding the celebration of feasts contributed to the improvement of the normally poor diets of large groups of people living below the poverty line. Over the centuries religion has had a profound influence on the dietary habits of the people. The present investigation was undertaken to study the influence of various religious rules and restrictions on the food choices and dietary patterns of the people in general and during pregnancy, lactation and childhood in particular.

The overview of these studies show that customs, beliefs, superstitions are highly significant in influencing the nutritional practices. Some of the above studies *(Maliha and Padma, 1976; Williams, 1973)* indicate that of major importance in the whole cultural background of the family are the beliefs, traditions, superstitions, taboos, attitudes, child rearing practices, religion and joint family system. They state that beliefs and practices are powerful factors influencing the nutritional status of the family members. Certain other studies *(Devadas, 1968; Gopalan, 1966)* state that each family develops its own pattern of serving meals. Customs and traditions of cooking and setting meals differ widely.

The present investigation undertook to study the various customs, beliefs etc., influencing the nutritional practices of people belonging to various religious communities, as any practice in a community is the product of social interaction deeply entrenched in the minds of the people with deep faith. To change poor dietary practices and improve the diets, it is essential to study the influence of taboos, beliefs and customs.

Social Factor

The social status attributed to certain foods may be much more important to people than any nutritive value it contains.

Fleck and Munves (1962) reported that foods like Persian Caviar or Pheasant under glass have a high social status. In some areas of America if a food is packaged, wrapped or preserved in some manner, it has greater status. Certain persons feel that foods purchased directly from the source of supply as in the case of fruits and eggs from the farm have a particular value. On the other hand, people who live on farms often place a high value on foods from the city. Most imported foods have special value to Americans. In this way they can identify themselves with a social status superior to their own. Some persons who have improved their socio-economic status may feel insecure and offended if offered with food which they consider low in status, such as boiled cabbage or hamburger. These, or other foods may remind them of poverty or certain aspects of low levels of living, such status foods vary from one country to another.

Moore (1952) points out that American foods become hoity-toity, if they are rare, expensive exceptionally difficult to prepare or frequently liked or extreme in flavour or taste qualities. Thus food is used as an indication of one's social sophistication, powers and gentility.

Prestige demands that one should have rare and costly items of food. *Devadas (1968)* reported some of the social values of foods in India. Whatever is grown in abundance or available free of cost like drumstick leaves or cheap as in the case of greens, papaya, plantain and amla is regarded with disdain, because it is plentiful. Even when such foods possess high nutritive value, they are not acceptable. Because of prestige, white rice is prefered to brown par-boiled rice, sugar to jaggery, hydrogenated fat to gingelly or groundnut oil, bengal gram to horse gram. The standard of living and the status of a family is judged from the quantity and quality of its food and dietary habits. In the march of fashion tea and coffee have come to be widely used.

She also indicated that prestige stands in the way of accepting new practices and to change food habits. People want to emulate the elite those whom they consider superior, occupying high social positions and the cinema stars. In Mysore, ragi, which was once ridiculed as poor man's food is now accepted widely because His Highness the Maharaj Krishnaraja Mudaliar eats ragi at every meal.

Rao (1966) reported from the studies conducted in Telangana villages, that the mid-day school lunch programme has not been received very kindly by some of the prestige conscious villagers. "Why should our children eat the yellow corn or maize upma and drink powdered milk when we produce the best rice and possess the highest milk yielding buffaloes in the village?" Is the constant refrain one hears. This is the prestige factor for them.

The food distribution in the family depends upon the status and role and interpersonal relationships among the members of the family rather than on their nutritional needs. *Rao (1966)* reported that in Telangana region of Andhra Pradesh the senior and earning wage earners are served first and are also given the best diet both in quantity and quality while the vulnerable segments namely the children and women of child bearing age get the left overs, with the exception of milk, biscuits and other such items which are usually given to children.

Nutritional practices are influenced by social factors also. Social status attributed to certain foods may be much more important to some people than the nutritive value attributed to foods. Foods used are an indication of social sophistication, and gentility. An overview of above studies shows that prestige demands that one should have rare and costly items of food. The standard of living and the status of a family judged from its nutritional practices and prestige stands in the way of accepting new practices and change in food habits. The present investigation also assessed the influence of social factors on nutritional practices in attempt to help living about change in poor dietary habits.

Ecological Factors

Individuals and populations do not live alone in nature but in association with other organisms in an abiotic environment. There exists as net work of relationship of each and every part, living and non-living. Such a community of plants and animals together with the environment that controls it, is called an eco-system. An eco-system is made up of two large parts. The physical environment and the biological community. The physical components of a typical natural eco-system are: energy, water, atmosphere, fire, gravity, topography, geological substraction and soil. The biological factors are green plants, non-green plants, animals and man. The physical environment provides the energy, raw materials and living space that the biological community needs and uses for its growth and maintenance. In this context, it can be stated that a number of ecological factors—(a) Availability of food, (b) Geographical location, (c) Floods, famines and wars, (d) Industrialisation and urbanisation influence the nutritional practices of various groups.

Availability of Food

One of the principal factors affecting food choices is availability. For most of the United States and Canada wheat is the grain mostly because it can be grown in abundance and is available in plenty. Rice is the grain eaten in Southern China because it will grow in that area while other grains do not (1951). It appears that money alone does not explain the better diet of the economic classes. Greater availability of food is one of the additional factors.

Geographical Location

Aykroyd (1968) indicates that geography or locality naturally influence food patterns. Since rice but not wheat, flourishes in South East Asia, the inhabitants of that region are in general rice eaters, rather than wheat eaters.

Prugh (1961) indicates that as the geographic and social mobility of families and individuals has increased in democratic societies, a number of shifts in cultural attitudes towards food and eating have taken place, particularly under conditions of abundance.

India is a vast country with variable climates and geographical conditions which greatly influence the food availability, food habits and hence the nutritional status of its people.

Burgess and Dean (1957) pointed out that adequate facilities for the storage and transport of foods, preservation of surplus food, and marketing help to make the best use of the food supply of the country.

Valassi (1962) says that "The food habits of an immigrant may be partly explained on the basis of the climate and agricultural production of the country".

Thus it may be said that geographical location influences the dietary habits of groups to a certain extent.

Floods, Famines and Wars

Shortages which come about through wartime, flood, or famine pressures may develop longings for certain foods or place a high value on others. During wartime citizens are challenged to make adaptations for foods which are scarce which are needed for the war effort. When particular foods are reduced in availability or are omitted completely, it is necessary to consider substitutes. Therefore, war, famines, and flood also affect food habits of people.

Devadas (1968) indicates that failure of supplies, black-marketing, hoarding, adulteration and breakdown in the distribution machinery are some of the problems during war and the consequent food shortage periods. Due to the needs of the defence personnel, food distribution to the civilians is affected in terms of net availability. Rationing was introduced during world war II and this restricted food supply brought about a salutary change in food habits. In the South people who had never used wheat have started liking it because it was included in the rations.

Industrialisation and Urbanisation

The development of industries has drawn more and more of the agriculturists to the cities and towns, upsetting the normal agricultural cycle. It has lead to urbanisation which in turn has stimulated the growth of each crop, economy, leading to impoverishment of the soil and considerable reduction in food crops. On the other hand, growth of transport and communication facilities have brought in greater varieties of new foods from distant places, within the reach of the rural and urban home makers. This inturn has brought about many changes in the food habits of people.

Bageli et. al., (1964) studied the dietary habits in a rural area near Calcutta and in the city of Calcutta. He found that rural families spend 92 per cent of the total income on food whereas the urban families spend around 58 per cent. This difference was found to be due to a difference in expenditure pattern. In the rural areas, expenses for items other than food are negligible as compared to the amount spent for food, whereas in the urban areas expenses like rent for living rooms, clothing, education for children, amusements etc., pile up to about 35 per cent of the total expenditure. The investigators observed food attitudes and food habits especially related to infant feeding and pregnancy and found that in rural areas women were more tied down by rigid customs regarding dietary habits, whereas those in the urban areas, were comparatively flexible. Another distinct difference was the strong tendency among the poor urban families to consume foods of prestige value such as sugar, biscuits, lozengers, bread, tea, etc., while their rural counterparts consume puffed rice, jaggery, chapathi and seasonal fruits. In the urban families rigid dietary restrictions do not exist possibly due to the reasons that the mothers have less time. Secondly the arey influenced by cultural practices from various other communities and other economic groups.

Basel (1965) has pointed out the following factors which influence the food habits of people in urban areas.

1. The temptation or necessity for women to leave their children to another's care while they enter the "pay for hire world".

2. Introduction of milling equipment for cereal grains traditionally eaten in an undermilled state.

3. A shift away from breast feeding.

Degarine (1960) states that rapid social changes taking place as a result of urbanisation influence habits which mostly affect food.

Among urban groups, cessation of breast feeding is occurring much earlier than was traditional. *Jelliffe (1962)* says that this is due to two main sometimes interrelated reasons.

1. A need for the mothers to go out to work all day, and

2. A real or imaginary adequacy of lactation due to the pressure of a complex of social factors.

Rao and his colleague (1966) in their investigation found out that "permissive breast feeding was carried out uneventually and was continued for 2 to 3 years. They noted that there was a tendency to stop breast feeding earlier in urban areas.

The diet atlas of the *Indian Council of Medical Research (1951)* which is based on a large number of sample studies in all states, provides ample evidence that urbanization has a beneficial effect on the diet, resulting in a higher consumption of protein, vitamins, fats and fewer cereals.

According to *Burgess and Dean (1962)* some causes of malnutrition are:

1. The man of the rural family may be driven to seek work in the towns, with a subsequent deterioration

in the amount and quality of the foods that are grown in the rural areas.

2. Women or mothers may be forced to become wage earners. So children will be weaned early and left inadequately fed during the day light hours.

To conclude, because of urbanisation and sophistication the possibility of obtaining an adequate diet from local sources will become less. As most villages are getting semi-urbanised and urbanised the impact of urbanisation on food habits of people living in India is more.

An overview of the above studies indicates that ecological factors certainly influence dietary habits. Geographical location, availability of food including facilities for storing, processing and transporting of food, scarcity of food due to famines, floods, wars and urbanisation—all influence the nutritional practices of various groups.

Psychological Factors

Knowledge of the emotional value of food is of course, much older than knowledge of its nutritive value, both in the historical and in the individual biologic organism. One of the most primordial of human urges was that of eating. When pre-historic man foraged for food, he did so to satisfy his urge to eat and to survive and not to satisfy his nutritional requirements. Food is even more meaningful to people today as a symbol of love and gratification, as a sign of emotional identification. Food may even serve as a weapon of interpersonal warfare between giver and receiver. From childhood food is treated as a symbol of emotional value rather than as a source of calories. In the infant, food intake is usually associated with love, protection, pleasure and comfort.

Mead (1953) his said "In the most societies, food is the focus of emotional association, a channel for interpersonal relations for the communication of love, discrimination or disapproval. It usually has a symbolic reference.

Ritchie (1957) indicates that food may be closely associated with feelings of security beyond that of providing nourishment for the body. Familiar foods give a feeling of security, conversely, lack of an accustomed food that is associated with orderliness in daily life can cause anxiety and tension.

Proudfit and Robinson (1965) also says that food is a symbol of security to many. Milk the first food of the infant, may be associated with the security of the infant held lovingly in his mother's arms. A person may be away from home or may be ill, and looks upon milk as expressing the comfort and security of the home. Milk might be refused because the individual drinking it he does not want to admit his feelings and so says he does not want to be treated like a baby.

Hargog (1962) reported that in Holland a group of Indonesians showed great enthusiasm in the first instance about belonging to the Netherlands community, demanding Dutch food and dressing in European clothes. When however, difficulties arose with the Netherlands government they felt insecure and somewhat resentful and they changed back to their own food, though they continued the other European habits they had adopted. Emotional insecurity therefore affected their food behaviour more than it did the other practices.

Fleck and Munves (1962) indicates that the meanings people attach to food have a great effect upon their eating habits. The family attitudes may be quickly transmitted during meals. If a mother is worried about the cost of food, resents the amount of time it takes to prepare or feels that it is not accepted or appreciated by her family, these attitudes will be absorbed by the others at the table and have an indirect effect upon the way they feel about the food before them. They also indicate that the food is used to relieve tension. When persons are worried, afraid or concerned in some manner, they may eat more food than usual. The food in itself usually gives little pleasure but individuals claim the emotional disturbance is eased. It may be an urge to return to the foods of infancy or childhood for a feeling of security or good habits may be altered in other ways to case the tension.

Moore (1952) has pointed out that foods and dishes are commonly categorized as rewards, punishments or illness by the housewife who prepares and serves them. She has no difficulty in communicating her affection and warmth to her family by the meal she places before them. So, housewife may use food as a weapon as a technique to punish, reprimand or engage. She can manipulate and influence her family by the foods she serves them. Thus Moore refers to food as an "unspoken language".

Martin (1963) and *Ginsburg (1952)* believe that eating is complicated in a psychological manner which begins in early infancy and lasts throughout life.

Eppright (1947) in a study of food preferences of Iowans discovered, that people generally were unable to analyse in a discriminating manner, why they liked or disliked certain foods. The knowledge that a food promoted health did not enhance its popularity.

Lewin (1942) indicates that food moves step by step through channels before appearing on the table. The psychological forces and the economic state influence the movement. If food is expensive, two forces of opposite directions are met in the housewife. She is in conflict. The force, away from spending too much money, keeps the food from going into a channel. A second force corresponding to the attractiveness of the food tends to bring it into that channel.

Burgess (1962) indicates that a person eats a certain food because he likes the taste, but that includes many qualities, such as the smell, the roughness or smoothness, the temperature or colour, the dryness, softness or hardness, many of which may be important to the individual.

Fleck and Munves (1962) indicate that tremendous emotional stress upon victims of disasters is sometimes associated with the food served to them at that time. This may affect their future attitudes toward those foods leading to non-appreciation of certain foods.

Proudfit and Robinson (1965) state that eating has usually emotional associations for human beings. Their attitudes towards foods are bound with the manner in which they were taught, what and how to eat as children or with memories of happiness or unhappiness. Likings for certain foods can be the result of satisfying hunger and of emotional relationship between children and those who feed them.

One can therefore conclude that everyone has had the experience of seeing someone who was very unpleasant before a meal and of changing one's attitude when presented with a food one liked very much in the past. Thus, psychological factors play a significant role in the food habits of people.

The studies, cited above highlight the fact that from childhood itself food is treated as a symbol of emotional value rather than as a source of calories. Food intake is associated with love, protection, pleasure and comfort. In most societies food is the focus of emotional association, a channel in interpersonal relations for the communication of love, discrimination or dis-approval. Food usually has a symbolic reference. However, psychological factors though important have not been studied in the present investigation as they are beyond its scope.

Other Factors

In addition to the above reviewed factors there are certain others which also exert their influence on the dietary habits of different groups. They are education, knowledge in nutrition and population.

Education

Education and enlightenment are the best vehicles of a desired change. A change in people's attitude towards health and disease is most important if any lasting changes for the better have to be brought about in their food habits. A child at school is the best teacher at home. A school lunch programme and the accompanying education could go a long way in diffusing those ideas to the child's home—children at school could take to small scale farming in vegetables and fruits and be explained their importance in the menu. Schools can also make children part of the shopping group for the dairy products or other products from the grocers and have the teacher explain their significance on the spot. Children then can be persuaded to use those principles of nutrition at home with their evening meals or over the weekend. Most parents modify their meals and go along with children's tastes and likes. In this manner the school could effectively modify the food habits or popularize a new product for its nutritional value. Education in fundamentals of nutrition can also help to educate the parents. A mother, somewhat informed about nutrition, will not use money to buy a soft drink for her baby and will instead invest it in milk. Education is important for the people to have good aims. Educational process may include things like providing practical suggestions for preparing foods in attractive ways. But while doing so, one must respect the likes and dislikes of a person or a community associated with a culture. It is very unwise to teach attractive beef preparations to a member of a Hindu community and pork preparations to a Muslim.

Food habits and taboos are forms of group and not mere individual behaviour. Their alteration can therefore be achieved only by education. Since the family is the basic unit in society, education must be aimed at it and reach all its members *(Teulon, 1968)*.

As Martin (1963) states "food habits do not spring full blown. They are gradually developed from infancy through childhood". Nutritionists need to be aware of the religious values, customs, beliefs, tradition-bound attitudes and practices which compose the total cultural pattern of any community *(The National Research Council—NRC, 1943:* and *Yudkin and McKenzie, 1964).* Our programmes of nutrition education need to operate within the framework of people's ideas and aspirations expressing utmost respect to their views. The approaches should highlight the beneficial components of the existing practices in order to remove indirectly, the harmful ones. Scientific information can be made acceptable by clothing them in the comfortable guise of local customs.

Knowledge in Nutrition

In most developing countries the problem of malnutrition is not due to lack of food, as much as lack of knowledge about the foods that are available and frequently this is made more grievous by harmful traditions.

Yudkin (1964) indicates that "Nutrition education" may become an important tool in modifying food choice in the future but only if we try to answer questions and accept the limitations which confine it at the moment.

In Israel food surveys by *Jhonston and Mellon (1960)* have shown that new settlers slowly adjust to their adopted country's food patterns, good and bad but that desirable changes are measurably faster among those families exposed to the national nutrition education programme through schools and welfare centres.

Wilson and Lamb (1968) studied food beliefs of American women in order to demonstrate that the food choice would not be affected by economic stress but more by education. They found that participants whose education includes home economics and nutrition did not accept the food fallacies accepted by their peers in other disciplines. Their correct beliefs about food could be attributed to education in home economics and nutrition.

Population

Malnutrition and uncontrolled fertility are phenomena of worldwide concern and they are closely interrelated. More babies mean more mouths to feed, with consequent malnutrition when food is scarce. Ill-fed families have high net reproduction despite high pregnancy wastage.

The greatest source of development of a nation is its people. India has the second largest population in the world (15 per cent) with 684 millions, although she occupies only 2.4 per cent of the world's land area. In India nutritional deficiencies are widely prevalent due to the low socio-economic levels of the majority of the population and the resultant inadequate consumption of foods. The vulnerable groups of pre-school children are particularly affected apart from the women, who are subjected to frequent pregnancies on subsistence level of nutrition.

Children below the age of five years, who constitute a major vulnerable segment of the population account for over 15 per cent of the population of India. About 40 per cent of total deaths in India occur in this age group as compared to 3 to 8 per cent in advanced countries west *(Census of India, 1969, Health Statistics of India, 1950).*

While many factors are known which affect the growth of children adequate nutrition is basic. Children who are undernourished or malnourished when they do survive, do not grow satisfactorily. The growth of the baby as well as adult height depend to a large extent on dietary intake during growth period although heredity also plays a role.

Children in large families are more affected by this problem than their counterparts in the smaller family. The smaller the family, the better is the nutritional status.

Limitation of family size increases the quantum of food available to each member of the family. Limited income is better utilized when the family size is small. The caloric and protein intake and nutritional status of 125 pre-school children from families of varying size reveals that children from the families of small size (below 5) had a better nutritional status in terms of height and weight then children from the large sized families (above 5). The children from small sized families had leaser evidence of clinical deficiency than children from large families.

Nutritionists have produced a rich literature on the effects of a woman's nutritional status on menstruation, ovulation, and the likelihood of conception (*Frisch, 1974* a,b in press; *Fresch and Revelle, 1971)* as well as on the course and outcome of pregnancy *(Hillman and Hall, 1968, Chopra et. al., 1970, Habicht et. al., 1973, NAS, 1973).* Serious complications of pregnancy, delivery and puerperium can be attributed to nutritional aberrations of women during pregnancy *(Berguer and Susser, 1970, Habicht et. al., 1974).* In a related sense, conginital malformation, birth weight, constitutional strength, defenses against diseases, growth and development and chance of survival of offspring may be significantly modified by the mother's prenatal nutritional state *(Albances, 1973; Klein et. al., 1973).*

All the above presented factors currently form a part and parcel of the government policies. Today, government feels that by improving educational levels and through it the knowledge of nutrition of the different vulnerable groups and by controlling the rate of growth of population through a number of policies, the nutritional status of its people can be raised. Thus many governments are concentrating their attention on these factors which exert their influence on dietary habits.

To sum up, poverty, large size family structures, cultural roots and the practices of the community at large, are formidable barriers in the special feeding programmes intended for mothers and children because 'neglecting' the adult males who are the wage-earners, providers and protectors and the older siblings in the family, break "family integrity". This must be noted in all efforts towards nutritional improvement of the vulnerable groups.

The above analysis reveals that in order to effectively plan and implement nutrition intervention programmes, the economic, cultural, social and psychological aspects must be integrated in a total approach.

3. Material and Methods

The main objective of the study was to survey and study the nutritional practices prevalent among families of different religious communities in Tirupati town. Food consumption patterns and a number of other factors influencing nutritional practices were assessed.

Selection of the Sample

A sample of families from different regions throughout the district or even the state would have been ideal. However, keeping in view the paucity of funds, time at one's disposal and a number of other factors, it was decided to choose the families of Tirupati town. Tirupati is a pilgrim town situated near Sri Venkateswara University campus and is a semi-urbanized area.

At the Municipal office of Tirupati, enquiry was made, to secure detailed information about the population in general and of the families in particular. Information about the total number of wards and the number of families belonging to different religions in the different wards was collected. Out of the twenty wards 650 families belonging to different religions were selected at random as sample population.

Sampling Procedure

The selection of a sample is governed by the purpose of survey, method of survey and the characteristics of the population *(Inana, 1944)*.

A statistically valid sample is of major importance in the evaluation of a group for different characteristics. Random sampling in which, each family has the same chance of being included in the study is useful for describing the larger universe, from which the sample is drawn. Keeping this in view, this investigator surveyed a total of 650 families selected at random. The sampling distribution as per the number of families per ward and as per religion is presented in Table—3.1.

Religious Groups Surveyed

India has the largest number of religious groups—Hindus, Muslims, Christians, Sikhs, Buddhists, Jains, Parsis and Jews as compared to those of other countries. Of these different religious groups, the present survey covered five religious groups. They are Hindus, Muslims, Christians, Sikhs and Jains.* Other religions could not be represented as their number was negligible in Tirupati town. These religious groups were studied in order to understand the role of religion in symbolizing, reflecting and enriching human life in a specific cultural and social setting with special reference to the nutritional practices of the people belonging to different backgrounds. Among the religious groups surveyed, while the Jains were lacto-vegetarians, the other religious groups consisted of both vegetarians and non-vegetarians. Due to this difference, in the chapter on Results and Discussion, while the food consumption and menu patterns of the religious communities—Hindus, Muslims, Christians and Sikhs were presented together that of the Jain community was presented separately.

---

* The sample consisted of 500-Hindu, 100-Muslim, 20-Christian, 20-Sikh and 10-Jain families.

Table—3.1 Distribution of Total Number of Families of Different Religions and Sample Size According to Wards

Ward No.	Jains		Sikhs		Christians		Muslims		Hindus	
	Total No.	Sample size	Total No.	Sample size	Total No.	Sample size	Total No.	Sample size	Total No.	Sample size
1	2	3	4	5	6	7	8	9	10	11
1	–	–	10	2	15	3	172	10	897	29
2	–	–	3	1	5	1	47	7	338	22
3	–	–	2	1	1	–	54	5	273	21
4	2	1	7	2	29	3	153	7	1093	28
5	–	–	4	1	3	1	29	7	441	26
6	–	–	5	1	35	5	187	8	1742	27
7	3	1	7	2	–	–	3	2	323	24
8	7	3	2	1	–	–	14	3	527	25
9	10	3	2	1	–	–	4	4	163	27
10	5	1	3	1	1	–	31	5	633	22

(Contd...)

(Table—3.1 Contd...)

1	2	3	4	5	6	7	8	9	10	11
11	–	–	3	1	–	–	2	2	323	24
12	1	1	–	–	3	1	23	3	550	26
13	1	–	6	1	5	2	162	7	784	25
14	–	–	3	1	–	–	18	4	792	25
15	1	–	–	–	–	–	5	2	268	22
16	–	–	5	1	–	–	10	5	446	21
17	–	–	2	–	–	–	33	5	407	27
18	–	–	3	1	3	1	24	3	1145	29
19	–	–	7	2	6	2	80	6	690	26
20	–	–	–	–	5	1	52	5	810	24
Total	**30**	**10**	**74**	**20**	**111**	**20**	**1103**	**100**	**12645**	**500**

Description of the Tool of Research

No one method has been found to be free of the errors and limitations, common to all researches conducted with human subjects. Therefore, any method used in a survey is open to criticism. Selection of a method or methods is frequently influenced by such factors as the purpose of the study, the size of the sample, characteristics of people to be studied and the availability of funds, personnel, time and equipment *(Inana, 1944)*. For the present investigation an interview-schedule was used.

The schedule for the interview needs to fulfil certain criteria such as simple vocabulary, straight forward questions and avoidance of questions of a suggestive nature. The schedule requires the presence of the interviewer and the interviewee at the same spot. For this a schedule of questions is prepared considering all the areas in which information is needed. The interviewer then administers the questions orally to the interviewee and notes the answers given.

The various nutritional practices of the sample population, the income and expenditure patterns for general items and food items and other related aspects were thus obtained.

The schedule covered the following aspects:

1. General information about the family, which included the details about the number of members, marital status, education and occupation of the family members, ventilation of the house, surrounding and type of house;

2. Health information including Infant and Child deaths;

3. The general economic conditions of the family covering income, expenditure and expenditure patterns on various foods;

4. Detailed information about the food and nutritional practices of the families belonging to different religious groups, of pregnant, lactating mothers and children.

Pretest was done to assess the clarity of the schedule and necessary corrections were made before finally administering it to the selected families. The number of families chosen for the pretest was 150.

Orr (1945) recommended that dietary and clinical surveys should be done along with budgetary surveys which will help to understand the economic conditions of the people and to suggest measures to overcome the deficiencies in their diets with the food available in the community within their budgetary restraints.

The present investigation covered in a limited way the budget for the food, the types of foods purchased, the diet consumed among different religious groups and the nutritional status of specific members of the family in relation to diet consumption patterns.

Data Collection

The duration of the survey was of five months from July to November, 1983. The questions were asked in Telugu the local language. The respondents were housewives. The answers were noted down in the proforma by the interviewer. Each interview lasted for about 2 hours. To collect correct information on the individual foods consumed, the investigator even spent 5 to 6 hours with some of the families, which were less responsive.

Type of Information

For each family the following information was collected:

1. Type of family (joint or nuclear), number of family members classified by age, sex, education,

occupation and by other physiological states like pregnancy and lactation;

2. General information on health conditions including infant and child deaths classified by type of illness and cause of death respectively;

3. Total income and expenditure pattern in general and the specific amounts spent on individual foods. For this the different food items were grouped under eleven groups of the cost of the foods under different groups was estimated;

4. The consumption pattern of different foods per day, week, fortnight and month was studied for all the 650 families belonging to different religions. These consumption patterns were classified for different religious groups under the different food groups;

5. Detailed assessment of the different methods of preparing foods was made. Information on cooking patterns including preparation practices such as washing and cutting of vegetables, amount of water used cook were also elicited;

6. Effort was made to find out the religious restrictions on the consumption of certain foods. Reasons for avoiding any foods were noted down. Foods prepared specially for festivals and occasions and the significance of cooking those particular dishes was also noted;

7. The food beliefs and superstitions existing among the various religious groups were studied. The food beliefs were further classified into heat producing, cold producing and flatulence causing as per the responses given;

8. Food practices that were followed during special conditions like pregnancy and lactation were noted.

Foods recommended and restricted during these special conditions were also probed into;

9. Information on infant feeding practices was obtained with special reference to bottle fed and breast fed babies and type of milk used;

10. Habits that adversely influence food intake were noted. Effort was made to find out if these habits had any influence on the nutritional practices of the population.

Evaluation of Data

Data related to the total food expenditure was evaluated by grouping expenditure on different foods into eleven groups. They are as follows:

Group	I	–	Cereals
	II	–	Pulses
	III	–	Vegetables
	IV	–	Fruits
	V	–	Meat and Fish
	VI	–	Eggs
	VII	–	Milk and Milk products
	VIII	–	Fats and Oils
	IX	–	Biscuits and Bread
	X	–	Sugar and Jaggery
	XI	–	Other foods (Nuts and Spices)

The percentage food expenditure pattern of the families belonging to the five religious groups was compared with each other. Within each religion, the highest and least percentage of expenditure on each of the food groups was observed. The families in general were classified according to their eating patterns, eating habits—vegetarian, non-vegetarian.

Data on religious restrictions on consumption of certain foods was evaluated by listing the various foods avoided by different religious groups. Food belief and superstitions followed by different religious groups were also listed in a separate table.

Infant feeding practices were studied by calculating the percentage of babies breast fed and bottle fed. The bottle fed babies were again classified into three groups depending upon the type of milk used to feed them. Amount per feeding (ml.) and the concentration of milk by age of the baby were also taken account of.

Food practices during special conditions like pregnancy and lactation were evaluated separately. Two tables were prepared one presenting specially recommended foods and the other presenting restricted foods during pregnancy and lactation.

Habits that adversely influence food intake were also noted.

Practical Problems in Obtaining Relevant Data

1. Though correct addresses of families were known, there was difficulty in tracing the locality since Tirupati is a fast developing town. Tirupati is also a semi-urban area, which is extensive as compared to a village in a rural area. Locating the families therefore took up considerable time.

2. Some housewives were employed and were not easily accessible for interviews. The investigator had to call more than once for an interview.

3. In most houses marketing is generally done by male members of the home. The housewife is therefore not aware of the expenditure pattern of foods. So, the investigator had to spend more time to approach the male member of the family as well as for the necessary information.

Practical Limitation

1. It was not possible to do a detailed nutritional survey on the vulnerable groups of a large sample of families as the time at one's disposal was limited.

2. Food analysis and bio-chemical assays were not done as time at one's disposal was limited.

3. The one day survey for food consumption did not give a true picture of non-vegetarian foods consumed among the families taking non-vegetarian foods. Some families have taken non-vegetarian items on the day of the survey while others have not.

4. Results and Discussions

Man's behaviour is not uniform. It differs from time to time and place to place. The differentiation is due to changes in various factors. It is commonly thought that people with different socio-economic and cultural characteristics tend to differ in their way of living and as a consequence even their food consumption and expenditure patterns differ.

From the past, all over the world, many nutritionists, eminent scientists and experts *(McKenzie, 1974, Poleman, 1973, Florencio, 1969; Devadas and Eswaran, 1971)* have stated that just as socio-economic factors influence man's life, so do cultural factors. The present investigation was undertaken to study the influence of various factors on nutritional patterns of communities with special focus on religion.

It is a known fact that every religion has to own special recommendations and restrictions on food habits. Some of these recommendations and restrictions are good from the point of view of nutrition, while others are quite harmful to health. Even in the progressive world of the present day, we come across people who adhere to their religion fanatically without going any rational thought. Therefore it was decided to undertake a study of nutritional practices among different religious groups.

The main objectives of this investigation were to study the nutritional patterns among different religious communities in Tirupati and the nutritional patterns of specific groups among these families namely pregnant, lactating women and children. The influence of other factors like income and education was also assessed.

General Living Conditions and Family Type

Man is inseparable from his surroundings and living conditions. The state of well being both physical, mental and social depends on his general living conditions. A glance at Table—4.1 shows the percentage distribution of families of different religious communities according to type of family and living conditions.

Regarding the type of family to which the various groups belong, it can be seen that more than half of them in all the communities are nuclear families, while a small percentage of Jains and Hindus belong to extended family type also. It is among the Christians (85%) that there are more nuclear families than among Muslims, Hindus and Sikhs. One may conclude that it is among the Jains that a large per cent of joint and extended families exist. This may probably be due to their unwillingness to divide properties.

With regard to the type of house, all the Jain families are living in cement constructed houses, with about three fourths of all the other communities also doing so. Only a small per cent of them live in tiled houses. About 10.20 per cent of them live in thatched huts with a majority of the Muslims doing so. This shows that even the type of house in which people live will give an indication of the status of the families. The findings of the study indicate that the Jains belong to the highest economic group.

Table—4.1 Percentage Distribution of Families of different Religious Communities as per Living Conditions

Religion	Type of Family			Type of house			
	Nuclear	Joint	Extended	Thatched	Shed	Tiled	Cement
Jain	50.00 (5)	40.00 (4)	10.00 (1)	–	–	–	100.00 (10)
Sikh	60.00 (12)	40.00 (8)	–	10.00 (2)	–	5.00 (1)	85.00 (17)
Christian	85.00 (17)	15.00 (3)	–	15.00 (3)	5.00 (1)	5.00 (1)	75.00 (15)
Muslims	75.00 (75)	25.00 (25)	–	19.00 (19)	7.00 (7)	8.00 (8)	66.00 (66)
Hindu	68.00 (340)	30.40 (152)	1.60 (8)	15.00 (75)	8.00 (40)	4.80 (24)	72.20 (361)

(Contd...)

(Table—4.1 Contd...)

Religion	Number of rooms					Lighting and ventilation			Location of the house	
	1	2	3	4	5 6 above	Poor	Moderate	Good	Healthy	Unhealthy
Jain	–	–	10.00 (1)	30.00 (3)	60.00 (6)	20.00 (2)	70.00 (7)	10.00 (1)	10.00 (1)	90.00 (9)
Sikh	10.00 (2)	25.00 (5)	25.00 (5)	20.00 (4)	20.00 (4)	15.00 (3)	60.00 (12)	25.00 (5)	60.00 (12)	40.00 (8)
Christian	5.00 (1)	25.00 (5)	30.00 (6)	40.00 (8)	–	5.00 (1)	55.00 (11)	40.00 (8)	80.00 (16)	20.00 (4)
Muslim	31.00 (31)	22.00 (22)	21.00 (21)	11.00 (11)	15.00 (15)	39.00 (39)	58.00 (58)	13.00 (13)	32.00 (32)	68.00 (68)
Hindu	24.00 (120)	16.60 (83)	18.40 (92)	20.20 (101)	20.80 (104)	33.00 (165)	46.20 (231)	20.80 (104)	62.20 (311)	37.80 (189)

The figures in paranthesis relate to number of families.

Majority of the houses under the occupation of Jains have five or more rooms, while only 15.20 per cent of the other communities with the exception of Christians are living in houses having more than five rooms. Most of the Christians are occupying houses with two, three or four rooms. Among the Muslims one third of them are living in a one room flat with about 20 per cent each living in two room and three room houses. The same type of situation is observed among the Hindu families. A quarter each of Sikh families are occupying two or three room houses. It is only among the Jains followed by a relatively small percentage of other groups that decent housing is existing. However, in the case of Jains, a larger percentage of the families are joint/extended families and therefore they require more rooms.

Taking lighting and ventilation into account, it can be seen that among all the groups, grade one marks can be given for good lighting and ventilation to Christians. However, about half or more of all the groups have moderate conditions and it is only one third of the Muslims and Hindus and a small percentage of the other communities who are having poor lighting and ventilation in their homes.

Concerning the 'location of the house', a majority of the Jains and Muslims are living in unhealthy surroundings. It may be surprising to note that Jain families who have a better economic status compared to others are living in unhealthy surroundings, but this is so because most of the Jains are businessmen and they have their houses behind their shops, which are all located in the Bazar street, a busy shopping centre of Tirupati. These unhealthy surroundings may lead to a higher incidence of illness among the Jain and Muslim families.

The living conditions of the various religious communities in general indicate that a large per cent of the Jains and Christians are well off compared to the other religious communities. A large per cent of the Jains belong to joint and extended family system while a predominant number of Christians belong to nuclear families. Majority of the Jains live in cement constructed houses with more than five rooms, while most of the Muslim and Hindu families live in one or two or three room flats. The Jain joint family system may have necessitated their living in large houses which was also possible due to their higher economic status facilitated by undivided properties. Lighting and ventilation, in all the communities were above average. Many of the Muslim and Jain families are living in unhealthy surroundings which can adversely affect their health status. The Christian and Hindu families have better surroundings.

Health Conditions

A study of the health conditions of the population is essential as this data will be useful in providing the means for more accurate anticipation of demands for various types of medical facilities and for specialized medical and health personnel. Also a study of the health needs of the population is necessary for planning of programmes closely related to health such as sanitation services etc.

Health condition of the families among different religious communities is presented in Table—4.2. Table—4.2 reveals that a large number of the children among Jains (50%), 34 per cent of children among Muslims and 20 to 25 per cent of children in the other religious communities have incidence of illness of one type or the other. A small percentage of adults among Muslim and Hindu religious groups and 30 to 40 per cent of the Jain, Sikh and Christian adults report illness. The children of jain and Muslim families have a greater incidence of illness compared to those of other religious groups.

Among the children, it can be observed that in all the groups, majority of them suffer from common colds and fever. However it is among the Jain, Sikh, Muslim and Hindu

Table—4.2 Morbidity of the Families Among Different Religious Communities

Religion	Illness incidence percent		Name of the illness									
			Common cold and cough		Fever		Diarrhoea/ dysentery		Infectious Hepatitis		Any other	
	Child	Adult	Children	Adults	Children	Adults	Children	Adults	Children	Adults	Children	Adutls
Jain	50.00 (5)	30.00 (3)	10.00 (1)	10.00 (1)	20.00 (2)	10.00 (1)	30.00 (3)	10.00 (1)	–	–	–.	30.00 (3)
Sikh	25.00 (5)	40.00 (8)	20.00 (4)	15.00 (3)	10.00 (2)	5.00 (1)	15.00 (3)	–	–	–	5.00 (1)	20.00 (4)
Christian	20.00 (4)	30.00 (6)	15.00 (3)	15.00 (3)	10.00 (2)	–	5.00 (1)	–	–	–	–	15.00 (3)
Muslim	34.00 (34)	6.00 (6)	20.00 (20)	1.00 (1)	29.00 (29)	5.00 (5)	16.00 (16)	–	–	–	–	4.00 (4)
Hindu	26.40 (132)	11.80 (59)	19.60 (98)	4.00 (20)	17.60 (88)	1.80 (9)	11.00 (55)	0.80 (4)	0.40 (2)	–	0.40 (2)	6.80 (34)

children that incidence of diarrhoea/dysentery is high. This may be especially due to their unhealthy living conditions.

A number of adults also are suffering from common colds and fever, while 20-30 per cent of them in Jains and Sikh families and 5-10 per cent of those of other religions suffer from miscellaneous illnesses like Blood Pressure, Diabetes, Ulcer, Heart trouble etc. A negligible per cent of families among the Hindus and 10 per cent of the Jains suffer from Diarrhoea/Dysentery. This is a clear indication of unhygienic conditions existing within or around the house.

Percentage number of deaths and causes for death among children in different religious communities is presented in Table—4.3. From the table, it can be seen that the highest of child deaths was among the Sikh families, while majority of them died due to unknown causes, about 15 per cent of them died due to diarrhoea/dysentery. A lesser per cent of the Jain, Muslim and Hindu families also experienced the trauma of infant mortality. Here also a large number of deaths were due to diarrhoea/dysentery. Among the Muslim and Hindu families, deaths also occurred due to fits, premature births and small pox. It is only among the Christians that child deaths occurred due to fever and premature births. There were no deaths due to diarrhoea/dysentery.

A small percentage of Hindu children died due to brain fever, while this did not happen in any other religious groups. Comparison of the various groups show that Hindu children died due to a variety of illnesses followed by Muslims. All the religious groups had child deaths due to diarrhoea/dysentery with the exception of Christians. It is surprising that Jains inspite of their relatively better housing and cleanliness are still subject to deaths due to diarrhoea/dysentary. This is most probably due to unsanitary conditions prevailing around their homes which should be improved.

Table—4.3 Per Cent Incidences of Deaths and Causes for Death Among Children in Different Religious Communities

Religion	*Per cent incidence of deaths	Causes for death						
		Fever	Diarrhoea/ dysentery	Fits	Premature	Small pox	Brain fever	Others
Jain	4.65 (2)	50.00 (1)	50.00 (1)	–	–	–	–	–
Sikh	8.11 (6)	–	16.67 (1)	–	–	–	–	83.33 (5)
Christian	2.82 (2)	50.00 (1)	–	–	50.00 (1)	–	–	–
Muslim	4.98 (26)	11.54 (3)	30.77 (8)	19.23 (5)	11.54 (3)	19.23 (5)	–	7.69 (2)
Hindu	3.89 (61)	29.51 (18)	21.31 (13)	8.20 (5)	9.84 (6)	4.92 (3)	6.56 (4)	19.67 (12)

* Incidence of death in relation to total number of children born in each community. The figures in parenthesis indicate the number of children that died.

Socio-economic Status of the Families

Man is a social being. He cannot live in isolation, without contacting other people and without following the norms within the community. In order to understand a community (the people in that community) all its socio-economic characteristics should be studied comprehensively. Socio-economic variables like education, occupation and income should be studied and cause effect relationship examined in order to find out the degree of development of a specific community. The following is a discussion of the socio-economic characteristics of different religious communities in Tirupati town.

Educational Status of the Women

Constitution of India proclaims the laudable objective of achieving free and compulsory education for all. This objective for universalizing education has augmented the pressure for its realization. In India, the most significant target group for educational planning is women population. The thrust of educational innovations have to be directed towards improving the quality of life of the population as a whole. In order to achieve this, it is essential to concentrate on women's lot as it is their influence which is exercised on all aspects of human life (social, religious, emotional, nutritional...) and is the major figure in household decision making.

In this investigation, women's education has special significance as they have considerable influence on the nutritional status of the family members. Educated women not only influence their own family but also bring about at progressive change in the community. Educated and emancipated women can plan better with regard to every aspect of family life including nutrition.

In the light of the above observations, information was gathered on the educational status of women of different religious communities. The related data is presented in Table—4.4.

Table—4.4 Per cent Distribution of Women Among Different Religious Communities as per their Educational Status

Educational Range	Jain	Sikh	Christian	Muslim	Hindu
Illiterate	–	15.00 (3)	–	50.00 (50)	24.00 (120)
1-5 class	60.00 (6)	20.00 (4)	10.00 (2)	30.00 (30)	20.40 (102)
6-10 class	30.00 (3)	40.00 (8)	10.00 (2)	13.00 (13)	28.80 (144)
+2 level	10.00 (1)	5.00 (1)	45.00 (9)	3.00 (3)	15.80 (79)
Graduation	–	15.00 (3)	35.00 (7)	3.00 (3)	9.00 (45)
Post-graduation (or) professionals	–	5.00 (1)	–	1.00 (1)	2.00 (10)
Total	**100.00** **(10)**	**100.00** **(20)**	**100.00** **(20)**	**100.00** **(100)**	**100.00** **(500)**

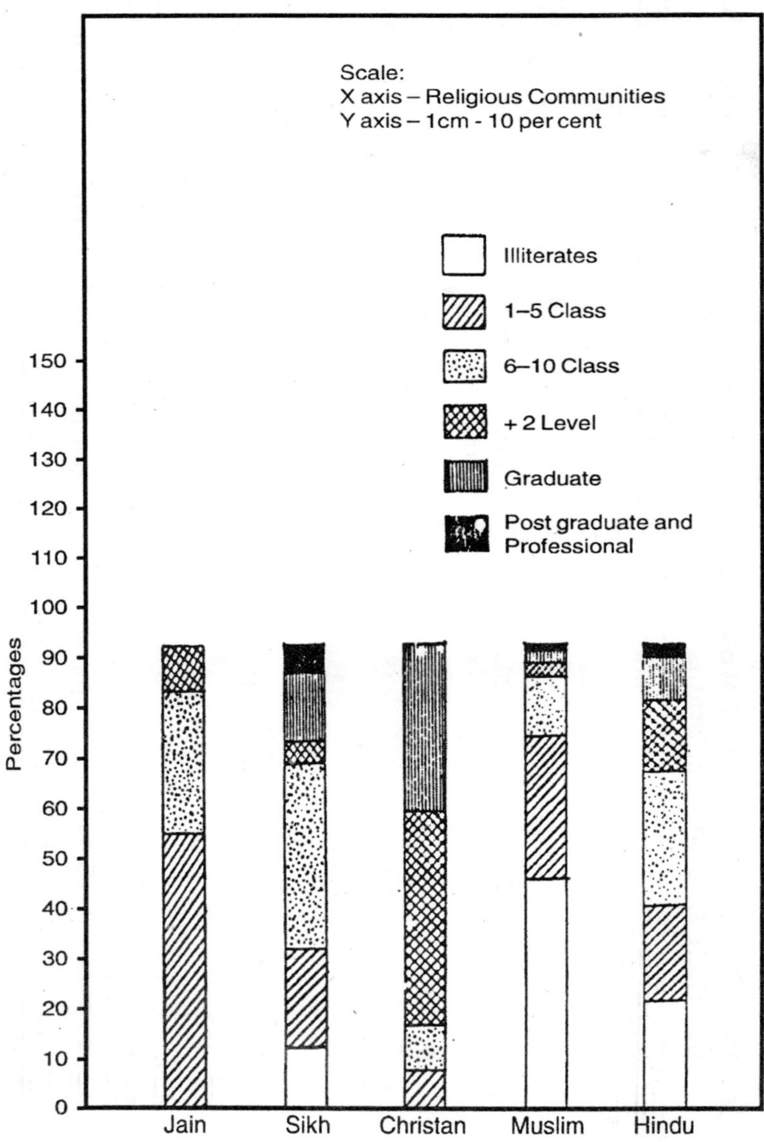

Fig.—4.1 Comparison of the Educational Status of Women of Different Religious Communities

The Fig.—4.1 highlights the extent of prevalence of illiteracy and the different levels of education among women in each of the religious communities.

In general with the exception of the Christian community, the majority of women have only school level education. The Jain women had only primary and secondary education. None of them had graduate education and infact only one of the Jain women had intermediate education.

There are some illiterates among Sikh women (15%). However 60 per cent of the women had primary and secondary school education while a few had plus two level education (5%). A small percentage of them (15%) were educated upto graduate level and 5 per cent of the women had Post-graduate education.

Among all the religious communities, it is the Christian women who are better educated and who also have a large percentage with collegiate education. There were no illiterates among them. No women had Post-graduate education.

It can be seen that illiteracy is prevalent to the extent of 50 per cent of the Muslim women interviewed. With the exception of Jain community, compared to Sikh, Christian and Hindu communities a large number of (30%) of Muslim women had only primary education. At the higher levels of education, an extremely small number of Muslim women are there. Only one woman had Post-graduation while another was graduate and three had education at plus two level.

In the case of Hindu women, it can be seen that eventhough a quarter of them are illiterate, still about 50 per cent have primary and secondary education. A few of them even have plus two level (16%), graduate (9%) and Post-graduate (2%) education.

At an overall level, the difference among the religious communities, illiteracy was prevalent among the Muslims,

Sikhs and Hindus while this was not the case with the Jains and Christians. The Jain women are exclusive in that there is neither illiteracy nor collegiate education prevalent among them. All of them have some education at the school level.

The Christian community of women can be said to be the most highly educated among all the communities. However, it has to be borne in mind that the size of sample studied is small for Christians, Jains and Sikhs as compared to that of Muslims and Hindus.

A Comparison of Educational Status of Men and Women

The educational status of men and women among different religious communities is presented in Table—4.5. In general with the exception of Christian community, majority of women have studied only upto school level while a large percentage of men have higher levels of education.

Among Muslims while illiteracy is prevalent to a greater extent of 50 per cent of the women, it is only 22 per cent in the men. A similar trend is observed among Hindu men and women. It is only among Muslims and Hindus that illiteracy is prevalent to a small extent among the men. However, at higher levels of education while an extremely small number of Muslim women were educated, considerable number of Muslim men had plus two level, Graduate and Post-graduate education, while Muslim men's educational status is higher than that of women there are very few among them who have had Post-graduate and/or professional education.

Among Hindus a considerable number of men have done Post-graduation as compared to women. In the Hindu women, while a quarter of them were illiterate, very few were so among the men. But 50 per cent of the women had primary and secondary education with very few having education above plus two level. Relative to the women, about 60 per cent of men had education above plus two level with considerable per cent of Graduates and Post-graduates.

Table—4.5 A Comparison of Educational Status of Men and Women Among Different Religious Communities

Education	Jain		Sikh		Christian		Muslim		Hindu	
	Men	Women	Men	Women	Men	Women	Men	Women	Men	Women
Illiterate	–	–	–	15.00	–	–	22.00	50.00	8.20	24.00
1-5 class	–	60.00	10.00	20.00	5.00	10.00	24.00	30.00	14.60	20.40
6-10 class	10.00	30.00	40.00	40.00	10.00	10.00	21.00	13.00	14.80	20.80
Plus two level	70.00	10.00	25.00	5.00	30.00	45.00	16.00	3.00	26.00	15.80
Graduate	20.00	–	5.00	15.00	35.00	35.00	11.00	3.00	18.80	9.00
Post-graduate (or) Professionals	–	–	20.00	5.00	20.00	–	6.00	1.00	17.60	2.00

All the figures are percentage values.

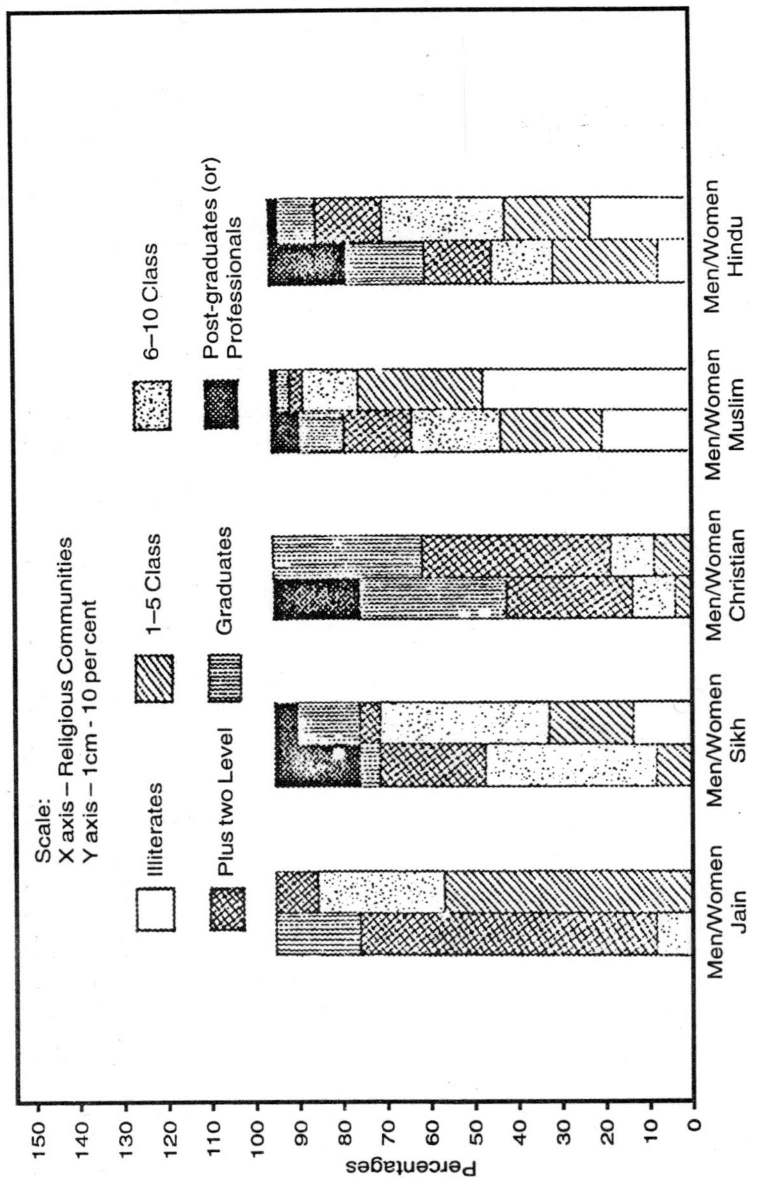

Fig.—4.2 Comparison of the Educational Status of Men and Women Among Different Religious Communities

Among the Jains neither the men nor the women had Post-graduate education while in all other communities a small percentage of them had Post-graduate or professional education. Among Jains, women had only primary and secondary education with only one having plus two level education. On the other hand, while a few of the men (10%) had secondary education, the remaining had plus two level and graduate education. However there were no Post-graduates among Jain men, while there were neither illiterates nor Post-graduates among the Jain women.

As in the case of Hindus and Muslims there are some illiterates (15%) among the Sikh women also. But there are no illiterates among the men. Almost equal number of men and women had primary and secondary education. While a small per cent of the women had plus two level education, a quarter of the men were educated upto plus two level. A small per cent (5%) of the Sikh men had Graduate education and 20 per cent Post-graduate education. In contrast, while 15 per cent of women had Graduate education only 5 per cent women had Post-graduate education. However, on the whole the educational status of both Sikh men and women is better than that observed among Muslims, Hindus and Jains.

Of all the religious communities, it is the Christians who have no illiterates and who have a large per cent with collegiate education both among men and women. Sixty five and eighty per cent of the men and women respectively have plus two and Graduate level education while 20 per cent of men have Post-graduate education. Since women been educated on par with men, it can be said that among Christians liberal views prevailed on women's education.

At an overall level, illiteracy is prevalent among the men and women of Muslim and Hindu communities only. Jains on the other hand have neither illiterates nor Post-graduates. Christian men and women are exclusive in that while there is no illiteracy, most of them are well educated.

Regarding the Sikhs, both men and women are fairly equally educated, at the school level, while at the Post-graduate level more men are educated than women (see Fig.—4.2). Generally men are better educated as compared to women.

Occupational Status of the Men

A commonly accepted vogue is that people with different occupations tend to differ in their standard of living and consequently there will be a difference in their food expenditure patterns. In order to study the influence of occupation on food expenditure patterns, it is necessary to have a clear picture of the occupational status of both men and women among families surveyed.

In the following discussion, various occupations of the men in the families studied have been grouped into six categories as follows:

1. Blue collar workers – Labourers, servants (household servants)
2. N.G.O. – U.D.C., L.D.C., Typist etc. (Non-gazetted officers)
3. G.O. and Professionals – Gazetted Officers, Doctors, Engineers, Lawyers etc.
4. Academicians – School and College teachers
5. Business – Jewellery, pawn brokers, cloth merchants etc.
6. Miscellaneous – Tailors, petty shop keepers, vendors etc.

The information collected is presented in Table—4.6

In order to effectively highlight the differences in occupational status of the men among various religious communities, Fig.—4.3 has been presented in page 78.

Table—4.6 Percentage Distribution of Men Belonging to Different Religious Communities as per their Occupational Status

Occupation	Jain	Sikh	Christian	Muslim	Hindu
Blue-collar workers	–	5.00 (1)	10.00 (2)	7.00 (7)	13.00 (65)
N.G.O.	–	10.00 (2)	25.00 (5)	9.00 (9)	28.00 (140)
G.O. and Professionals	–	20.00 (4)	–	4.00 (4)	12.40 (62)
Academicians	–	–	40.00 (8)	4.00 (4)	8.60 (43)
Business	100.00 (10)	40.00 (8)	–	21.00 (21)	15.80 (79)
Miscellaneous	–	25.00 (5)	25.00 (5)	55.00 (55)	22.20 (111)
	100.00 (10)	100.00 (20)	100.00 (20)	100.00 (100)	100.00 (500)

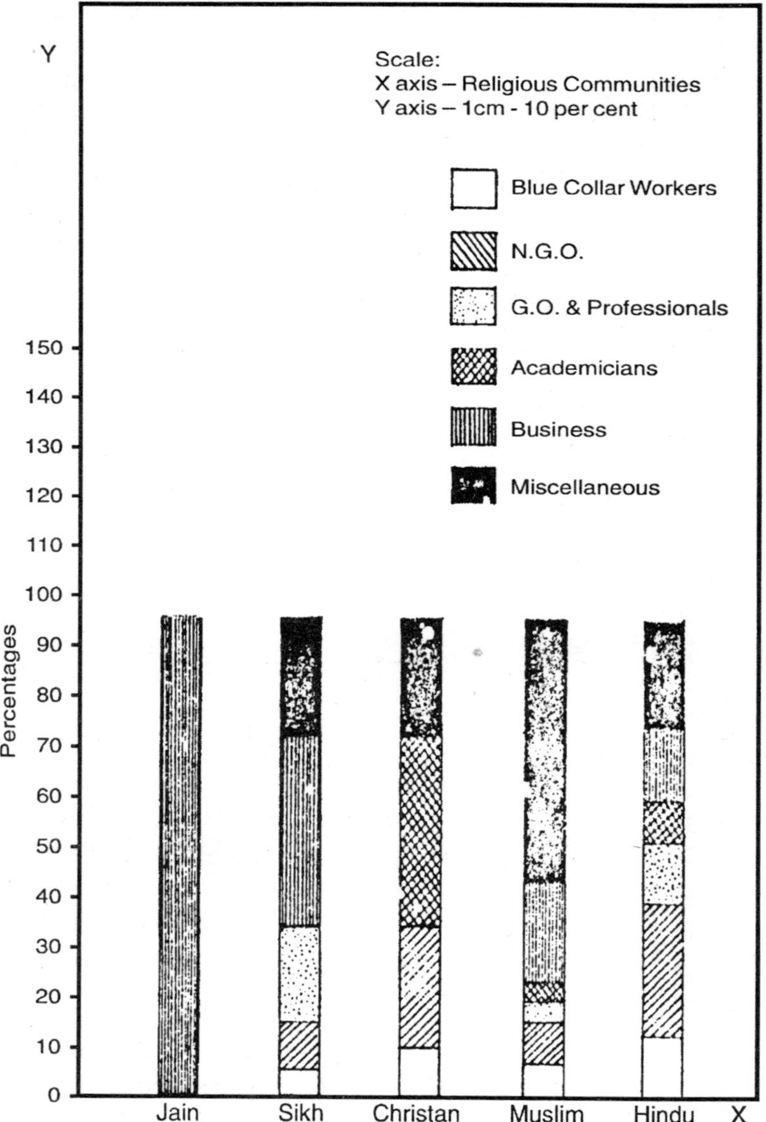

Fig.—4.3 Comparison of the Occupational Status of Men Among Different Religious Communities

Most of the men of Sikh, Christian, Muslim and Hindu communities are engaged in low income earning occupations, while all the Jains surveyed are engaged in business, a high income earning occupation. Jains are engaged in the sole activity of business of jewellery and pawn brokerage. Contrary to the general assumption that occupation is a consequence of education all the ten Jain families surveyed are in business, even though 90 per cent of the men are educated upto plus two and graduate levels. This is probably because business is their traditional occupation and the young men are introduced to it even as they are getting educated.

Forty per cent of the Sikhs are engaged in business like cloth merchants, stainless steel vessel merchants and such others. Unlike the Jains none of them have jewellery and pawn broker business. Thirty per cent of them are blue collar workers and of miscellaneous category. Since the Sikh men are fairly well educated (25 per cent have graduate and Post-graduate education), 30 per cent of them are either N.G.O. or G.O. or professionals.

It can be seen that more than 50 per cent of the Muslims are engaged in miscellaneous activities for their livelihood. A small number (21%) of Muslims are in business while a negligible percentage of them are G.Os and professionals. A few (9%) of the Muslims are N.G.Os, while another 7% are blue collar workers. Very low income earning occupational status of the Muslims relates very well to their low levels of education. Most of the men in this community are illiterate and very few are educated above plus two level. The consequence is that only a small percentage of the men are academicians, G.Os and professionals.

In the case of Hindus, it can be seen that 28 per cent of them are N.G.Os, and about 22 per cent are engaged in miscellaneous occupations. Similar to the men in the Muslim community, very few of the Hindu men are educated above the plus two level. However, relative to the Muslim

Community, there are more men who have higher levels of education and consequently more are engaged in high income earning occupations such as academicians, business, G.Os and professionals.

Of all the religious communities, it is the Christians who have no one in business and who have the large percentage (40%) in the academic field. This may be due to their high educational levels (85%) of them were educated to plus two level, Graduate and Post-graduate education). A small percentage of them are in miscellaneous occupations with 25 per cent of them employed as N.G.Os.

At an overall level among the different religious groups, Muslims and Hindus are having a low income earning occupational status. The Jains are exclusive in that, all of them are in business. The higher educational status of the Christians is reflected in their occupational status also. The same is the case with Sikhs.

Occupational Status of the Women

It is essential to examine the occupational status of women also, as it shows not only the earning capacity of women but also the social change that is taking place today and the change in the role and status of women in the society. In this survey it was observed that all women are engaged in household work, eventhough some of them are employed in other occupations. The occupational status of women was examined in detail as employed women contribute to their family income which helps not only in meeting both ends but also influences the family nutritional patterns.

Per cent distribution of women belonging to different religious communities as per their occupational status is presented in Table—4.7. In order to effectively highlight the differences in occupational status of the women of different religious communities Fig.—4.4 has been presented *(See page 82)*.

Table—4.7 Per cent Distribution of the Women of Different Religious Communities as Per their Occupational Status

Occupation	Jain	Sikh	Christian	Muslim	Hindu
Labourers	–	–	–	13.00 (13)	8.60 (43)
Pettyshop Business	–	–	–	4.00 (4)	2.80 (14)
N.G.O.	–	–	5.00 (1)	2.00 (2)	3.40 (17)
School teachers	–	5.00 (1)	35.00 (7)	2.00 (2)	4.40 (22)
Lecturers	–	–	–	–	1.20 (5)
Nurses	–	–	15.00 (3)	–	2.20 (11)
Doctors	–	5.00 (1)	–	–	1.00 (5)
Exclusively house-hold work	100.00 (10)	90.00 (18)	45.00 (9)	79.00 (79)	76.60 (383)

The occupational status of women shows that only 23 per cent of the total number of 650 housewives interviewed, are employed. The remaining are attending to household work. Taking the case of women in each religious community separately it can be seen that none of the Jain women are engaged in occupations other than household work. The influence of cultural factors is very great in Jain households. As per the dictation of their culture, Jain women generally do not undertake any occupation outside their home. Apart from the dictation of cultural factors other reasons for their staying at home may be that most of the Jain households

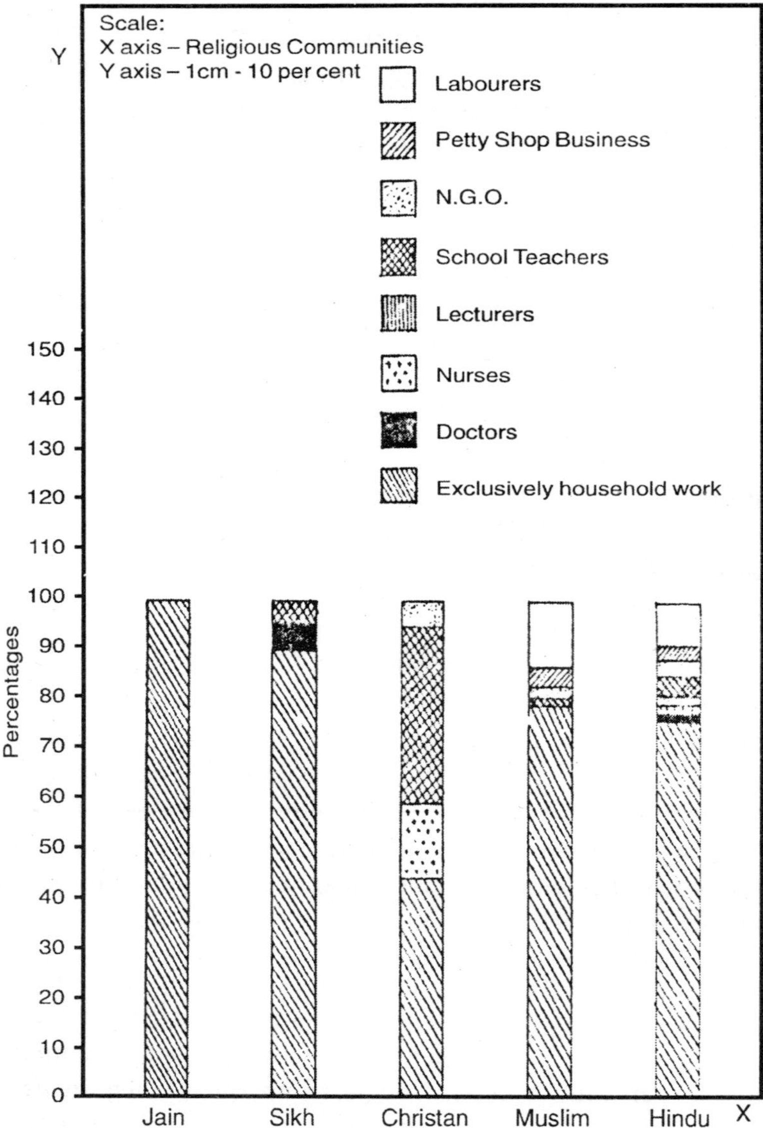

Fig.—4.4 Comparison of the Occupational Status of Women Among Different Religious Communities

are large joint families and each couple has a number of responsibilities in the house. Women in these families if they are engaged in work outside the house will not be able to cope with either their heavy household duties on the one hand or fulfil their job demands on the other hand. The educational status of all the Jain women is only that of school level and above all their financial status is sound. Hence, they feel it is not essential for them to work outside their home.

With regard to Hindu women the majority of them (77 per cent) are engaged exclusively in household work. While 23 per cent of them are in various other occupations such as labourers, petty shop owners, teachers and others. Among the Hindu women who are employed the occupational status of almost 50 per cent of them is low. It is observed that they also have low levels of education. However it is only in this community that a few women are employed as Lecturers.

Of the few Muslim women employed the majority of them (79%) are in low income unskilled occupations. A majority of the total number of working women are employed as labourers and in petty shop business with a negligible percentage working as either N.G.Os, or teachers. This is especially because of the high percentage of illiteracy and low levels of education of the women in this community along with cultural inhibitions.

In contrast the occupational status of the Christian women is high. Of the 55 per cent of the total number of Christian women employed, 35 per cent are teachers, 15 per cent nurses and 5 per cent N.G.Os. Compared to the women in Jain community who are all engaged in household work, majority of the Christian women are employed in fairly high income occupations. This may be related to their higher educational status. However, due to their middle economic status and large family size, the women tend to take up occupations mainly to supplement their family income. Apart from the above factors, the Christians have a liberal view regarding the education of women and many heads of the families encourage women's education. This attitude has naturally lead to higher education and to higher paid jobs for Christian women.

Two of the twenty Sikh women interviewed are in the high status occupations. One is a teacher and another is a doctor. The remaining eighteen women are housewives only. The two women employed are naturally highly educated. Illiteracy is prevalent among Sikh women also unlike the women in Jain and Christian communities. This may be one reason for many of the women to be involved exclusively in household work.

To sum up, Hindu women are employed in low paid diverse occupations. Majority of the Muslim women are engaged in low paid unskilled occupations. The Christian women are working in well paid jobs. All the Jain women are engaged in household work only. Only a small per cent of the Sikh women are working but their occupational status is high. The pattern of occupational status of women among different religious communities is closely related to their educational status as also cultural background.

Economic Status of the Families

It is a well known fact that economic status has a stronghold on the food habits and food intake of people in any community. People belonging to different income levels tend to be different in their expenditure patterns specially with regard to food. Those having lower economic status spend less on certain varieties of food, while people belonging to higher economic status tend to spend more on other varieties of food. To study the relationship between income and expenditure pattern on foods, the economic status of the respondents will be discussed.

In this survey, in order to assess the economic status of the families, data on annual income of the families is analysed. Based on the differential economic status of the families of different religious communities, income is categorised into the following six grades:

Grade I (5,000)

Grade II (5,001-15,000)

Grade III (15,001-25,000)

Grade IV (25,001-35,000)

Grade V (35,001-45,000)

Grade VI (45,001+)

Per cent distribution of families of different religious communities in relation to their income levels is presented in Table—4.8.

Table—4.8 Per cent Distribution of Families of Different Religious Communities as Per their Income Levels

Grade	Income level (per annum)	Jain	Sikh	Christian	Muslim	Hindu
I	≤ 5,000	–	5.00 (1)	–	5.00 (5)	16.00 (18)
II	5,001 – 15,000	20.00 (2)	50.00 (10)	25.00 (5)	64.00 (64)	37.80 (189)
III	15,001 – 25,000	20.00 (2)	30.00 (6)	50.00 (10)	24.00 (24)	22.20 (111)
IV	25,001 – 35,000	20.00 (2)	15.00 (3)	25.00 (5)	3.00 (3)	13.60 (68)
V	35,001 – 45,000	20.00 (2)	–	–	4.00 (4)	5.40 (27)
VI	45,001 +	20.00 (2)	–	–	–	5.00 (25)
	Total	**100.00 (10)**	**100.00 (20)**	**100.00 (20)**	**100.00 (100)**	**100.00 (500)**

In order to highlight the differences in economic status (income) of the various religious communities, Fig.—4.5 has been presented.

In all the religious communities a large percentage of the families belong to Grade II and III income levels. The percentage of the population belonging to Grades II and III is 40, 80, 75, 88, and 60 for Jain, Sikh, Christian, Muslim and Hindu communities respectively. It is only among the Hindus and Jains that a few families belong to Grade VI that is Rs. 45,001 and above. None of the families in other communities belong to it. Christians are exclusive in that none belong to either Grade I or Grades V and VI. Among the Jains with the exception of Grade I an equal number of families (20%) are in different income groups. Irrespective of income levels, all the Jains are engaged in business like jewellery and pawn brokerage. As a result of this there is no Jain family in Grade I category, which is less than Rs. 5,000 per annum.

Among the Sikh families, majority of them are in Grade II income group. A half of the number of Sikhs interviewed, fall in the Grade II (Rs. 5001-15,000) income category with another 30 per cent in Grade III. A small per cent are in Grade IV. Only one family falls in the category of less than Rs. 5,000 per annum. This family is engaged in vending of plastic goods. As has been already discussed, the occupation of the Sikhs is mainly small business like cloth merchants, stainless steel merchants and others. Hence the income of the majority of the families is between Rs. 5,001-25,000 per annum.

In the case of Christian community, majority of the families belonged to Grade III with a small number of them equally distributed in Grades II and IV. None of them are in either Grade I or Grade V and VI. Of the twenty families surveyed; ten belonged to the income groups Rs. 15,001—25,000 per annum. This middle income status is mainly due to

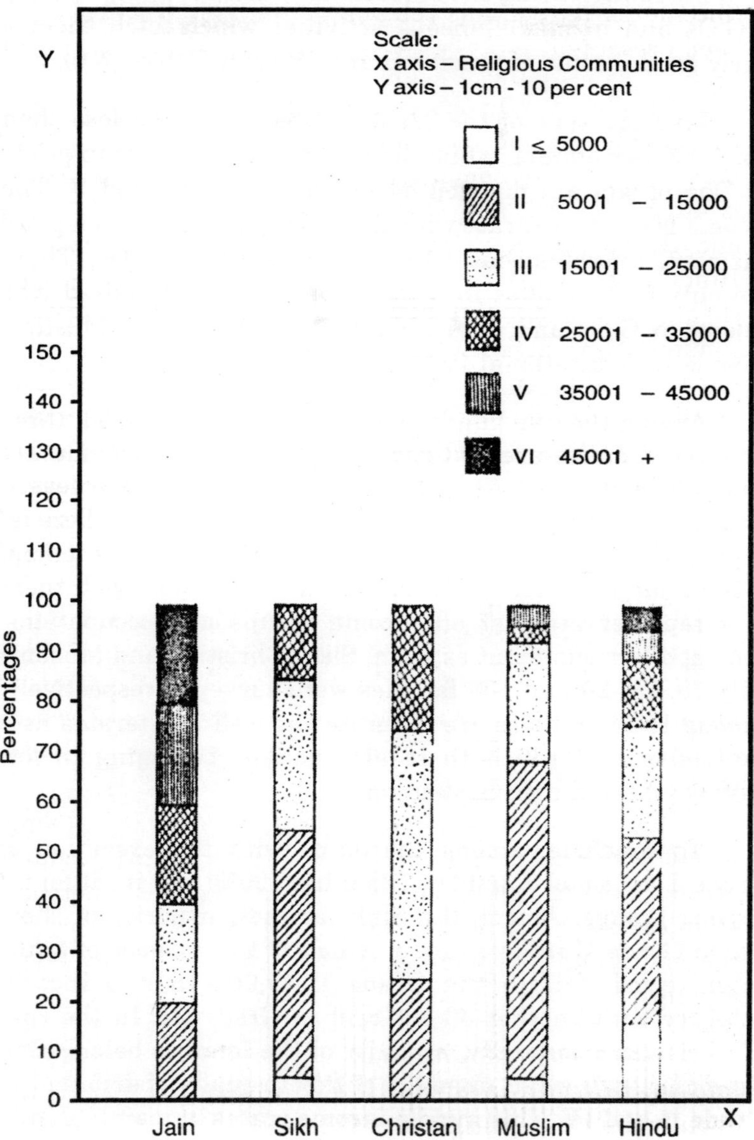

Fig.—4.5 Comparison of the Income Status of the Families Among Different Religious Communities

their occupation being one of teaching. Others are employed as N.G.Os and in miscellaneous activities which fetch them a fairly good income of Grades II and IV (vide Table—4.6).

Five per cent of the Muslims observed have less than Rs. 5,000 per annum, while the majority of them are in grade II. The others are distributed in grades III, IV and V. The income is commensurate with their occupations such as petty business, miscellaneous jobs, labourers and N.G.Os. There are only four families in a total population of hundred who belong to G.Os and professionals. Majority of the Muslims have lower educational status.

Among the five hundred Hindu families surveyed, three hundred families are at Grades II and III. This community has people in the lowest as well as highest income levels. This is the only community where people belonged to all grades of income. Similarly all occupations were represented. Since a large number of Hindu families was surveyed, there is a representation of all income groups and occupations. Among other communities, Jain, Sikh, Christian and Muslims only 10, 20, 20 and 100 families were surveyed respectively. Among Hindus, there are illiterates as well as literates as a consequence of which there are families belonging to low paying jobs and high paying jobs.

To conclude, among the Jains with the exception of Grade I an equal number of families (20%) are in different income groups. Among the Sikh families, majority of them are in Grade II income group. A half of the number of Sikhs interviewed, fall in the Grade II (5,001-15,000) income category with another 30 per cent in Grade III. In the case of Christian community, majority of the families belonged to Grade III with small numbers of them equally distributed in Grade II and IV. This middle income status is mainly due to their occupation being one of teaching. Five per cent of the Muslims observed have less than Rs. 5,000 per annum, while the majority of them are in Grade II. The others are distributed in Grade III, IV and V. The income is commensurate with their occupations such as petty business, miscellaneous jobs, labourers and N.G.Os. Among the five hundred Hindu families surveyed three hundred are in Grade II and III groups. This community has people in the lowest as well as highest income levels. This is the only community where people belonged to all grades of income.

Nutritional Patterns Among Families of Different Religious Communities

Total Food-expenditure Pattern as Related to Income

Food-expenditure pattern among different religious communities as per their income levels is presented in Table—4.9. *(See on Page 91-92)* The declining trend of expenditure of food with increasing income levels among different religious communities has been effectively shown in Fig.—4.6.

The findings of this survey agree with Engle's law which states that "as income increases, smaller is the relative percentage of the total outlay spent for food" (Fig.—4.6). Among the Jains the per cent expenditure on food declines from 52 to 32 with increasing income. The same trend can be noticed in the case of all the other religious groups. Among the Sikhs the expenditure decreased from 56 to 32, among Christians 56 to 38, among Muslims 66 to 39 and among Hindus 68 to 31 per cent.

The level of expenditure on foods differed from one income group to the other. Among the Jains, the per cent expenditure on foods of families belonging to Grades IV, V and VI is decreasing with increasing income in accordance with established evidence. However, in the Grade IV income groups, the per cent expenditure on food has increased to 49 from 45 in Grade III. In this particular income group, the mean family size was 10.5, which is higher than either 7.5 or 6.0 in Grade III and V respectively. This may be the reason for the higher expenditure in this particular income group (vide Appendix—III).

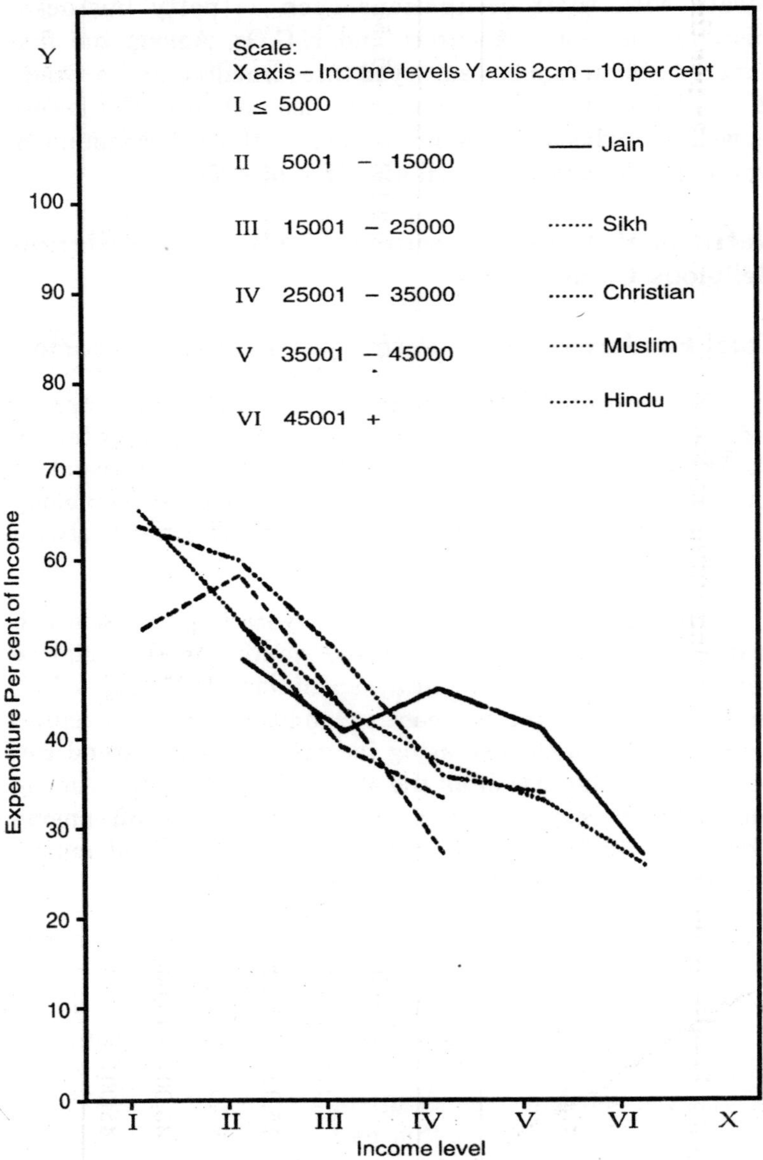

Fig.—4.6 Food Expenditure Trends in Relation to Income Among Different Religious Communities

Table—4.9 Food-expenditure Pattern Among Different Religious Communities as per their Income Levels

Grades	Income levels (per annum)	Jains			Sikhs		
		Income	Expen-diture	Per cent expen-diture	Income	Expen-diture	Per cent expen-diture
1	2	3	4	5	6	7	8
I	≤ 5,000	–	–	–	4,320	2,400	55.56
II	5,001 – 15,000	12,600	6,600	52.38	10,760	6,540	60.78
III	15,001 – 25,000	24,000	10,800	45.00	22,900	10,800	47.16
IV	25,001 – 35,000	31,800	15,600	49.06	30,800	10,000	32.47
V	35,001 – 45,000	36,000	16,200	45.00	–	–	–
VI	45,001 +	75,000	24,000	32.00	–	–	–

(Contd...)

(Table—4.9 Contd...)

Grades	Christians			Muslims			Hindus		
	Income	Expen-diture	Per cent expen-diture	Income	Expen-diture	Per cent expen-diture	Income	Expen-diture	Per cent expen-diture
I	–	–	–	4,080	2,700	66.18	4,209	2,856	67.85
II	9,000	5,040	56.00	9,098	5,662	62.23	10,212	5,688	55.70
III	18,900	8,280	43.81	19,763	10,425	52.75	19,395	9,216	47.52
IV	28,800	11,040	38.33	29,600	12,000	40.54	29,063	12,088	41.59
V	–	–	–	40,650	15,650	38.50	38,930	34,859	38.17
VI	–	–	–	–	–	–	60,792	18,792	30.91

All figures are mean values.

With regard to Sikh community, there is an increase in per cent expenditure on foods from 55 in Grade I to 61 in Grade II. However, after that the per cent expenditure on foods is decreasing from 60 to 32. Similar to the Jain community in Grade IV income group, Sikhs in Grade II also have a 6.3 mean family size relative to 4.0 and 5.83 in Grades I and III respectively. The larger family size may have resulted in higher expenditure at the Grade II level.

Among the Christians, Muslims and Hindus, the per cent expenditure on foods of the families in all the income groups is declining as income is increasing. However, the per cent expenditure on food of families belonging to Muslim community is more at all the income grades compared to that of other religious communities with the exception of the Jains in Grade IV income group. Particularly the per cent expenditure of food of Muslims in Grade II and III income groups is the largest as compared to that observed in all the other religious communities.

On the whole it can be observed that with an increase in income, the per cent expenditure on food of families in all religious communities tends to decline except in some exceptional cases where the size of the families represented is relatively larger. The results presented in Table—4.9 clearly reflect the inverse relationship between income and food-expenditure. *Burgess and Dean (1962)* explain that the levels of living depend ultimately on levels of income. In the lower income groups any rise in economic status is usually reflected in an increase in the quantity of food consumed with little change in quality. At even higher level increased income usually results in greater expenditure on quality foods such as meat, egg and milk products with a consequent improvement in the nutritive value of diets. The overall percentage expenditure however on foods decreases at the higher income level.

Expenditure Pattern on Different Food Groups as Related to Income

It is a well known fact that a large per cent of the income is spent on food in the lower income groups as against a relatively small per cent of the income in the affluent group. It has also been observed that, at higher income levels the quality of food consumed improves. *Devadas and Eswaran (1971)* noted that the economically better off consumed a variety of side dishes. They also showed that the percentage of food consumption and expenditure on protective foods like meat, fish and eggs increases with increasing income.

In order to know the type of foods and the amount spent on these with increasing income the expenditure has been calculated for each of the five food groups at each income level for the different religious communities. The information is given in Tables—4.10 to 4.14 for Jains, Sikhs Christians, Muslims and Hindus respectively. Among all the religious communities, the per cent expenditure on foods such as cereals, bread and biscuits and sugar and jaggery (Group I) is declining with increasing income *(See Fig.—4.7 on Page 105)*. With regard to all the other food groups the per cent expenditure is steadily increasing with increasing income levels. In the first food group, in accordance with established evidence *(Gopalan, 1967),* the per cent expenditure on cereals is decreasing as income is increasing, while the per cent expenditure on other food groups is increasing with increasing income.

The Jain culture prohibits the consumption of non-vegetarian foods and hence the Jains are lacto-vegetarians. In comparison with other religious communities it can be noted that the per cent expenditure on food groups III and V is more among Jains. Since they are lacto-vegetarians, there is a higher consumption of vegetables and fruits and milk and milk products.

Table—4.10 Expenditure Pattern on Different Food Groups as Related to Income Among Jain Families

Grades	Income level (per annum)	Actual total income	Actual expenditure on foods	Expenditure on foods per cent income	Food Groups			
					I		II	
					Actual expn.	Per cent expn. on foods	Actual expn.	Per cent expn. on foods
I	≤ 5,000	–	–	–	–	–	–	–
II	5,001 – 15,000	12,600	6,600	52.38	3,150	47.73	700	10.61
III	15,001 – 25,000	24,000	10,800	45.00	3,820	35.37	1,400	12.96
IV	25,001 – 35,000	31,800	15,600	49.06	4,590	29.42	2,150	13.78
V	35,001 – 45,000	36,000	16,200	45.00	4,080	25.19	2,400	14.82
VI	45,001 +	75,000	24,000	32.00	5,800	24.17	3,580	14.91

(Contd...)

(Table—4.10 Contd...)

Grades	Food Groups							
	III		IV		V		Other foods	
	Actual expn.	Per cent expn. on foods	Actual expn.	Per cent expn. on foods	Actual expn.	Per cent expn. on foods	Actual expn.	Per cent expn. on foods
I	–	–	–	–	–	–	–	–
II	800	12.12	890	13.49	600	9.09	480	7.27
III	1,700	15.74	1,600	14.82	1,450	13.42	980	9.07
IV	2,580	16.53	2,400	15.39	2,500	16.03	1,500	9.62
V	2,760	17.04	2,500	15.43	3,000	18.52	1,700	10.49
VI	4,350	18.12	3,800	15.83	4,500	18.75	2,450	10.20

All data is expressed as mean values

I group – Cereals, biscuits, bread, sugar and jaggery

II group – Pulses, meat, fish and eggs

III group – Vegetables, greens and fruits

IV group – Fats and oils

V group – Milk and milk products

other foods– Condiments and spices.

Table—4.11 Expenditure Pattern on Different Food Groups as Related to Income Among Sikh Families

Grades	Income level (per annum)	Actual total income	Actual expenditure on foods	Expenditure on foods per cent income	Food Groups			
					I		II	
					Actual expn.	Per cent expn. on foods	Actual expn.	Per cent expn. on foods
I	≤ 5,000	4,320	2,400	55.56	1,200	52.50	420	17.50
II	5,001 – 15,000	10,760	6,540	60.78	2,334	35.69	1,182	18.07
III	15,001 – 25,000	22,900	10,800	47.16	3,310	30.65	2,010	18.61
IV	25,001 – 35,000	30,800	10,000	32.46	2,880	28.80	1,880	18.80
V	35,001 – 45,000	–	–	–	–	–	–	–
VI	45,001 +	–	–	–	–	–	–	–

(Contd...)

(Table—4.11 Contd...)

	Food Groups							
	III		IV		V		Other foods	
Grades	Actual expn.	Per cent expn. on foods	Actual expn.	Per cent expn. on foods	Actual expn.	Per cent expn. on foods	Actual expn.	Per cent expn. on foods
I	300	12.50	180	7.50	180	7.50	120	5.00
II	948	14.50	606	9.27	788	12.05	774	11.84
III	1,840	17.04	1,020	9.44	1,600	14.82	1,280	11.85
IV	1,760	17.60	960	9.60	1,500	15.00	1,200	12.00
V	–	–	–	–	–	–	–	–
VI	–	–	–	–	–	–	–	–

Table—4.12 Expenditure Pattern on Different Food Groups as Related to Income Among Christian Families

Grades	Income level (per annum)	Actual total income	Actual expenditure on foods	Expenditure on foods per cent income	Food Groups			
					I		II	
					Actual expn.	Per cent expn. on foods	Actual expn.	Per cent expn. on foods
I	≤ 5,000	–	–	–	–	–	–	–
II	5,001 – 15,000	9,000	5,040	56.00	2,148	42.62	892	17.70
III	15,001 – 25,000	18,900	8,280	43.81	3,070	37.08	1,598	19.30
IV	25,001 – 35,000	28,800	11,040	38.33	3,128	28.33	2,412	21.85
V	35,001 – 45,000	–	–	–	–	–	–	–
VI	45,001 +	–	–	–	–	–	–	–

(Contd...)

(Table—4.12 Contd...)

Grades	Food Groups							
	III		IV		V		Other foods	
	Actual expn.	Per cent expn. on foods	Actual expn.	Per cent expn. on foods	Actual expn.	Per cent expn. on foods	Actual expn.	Per cent expn. on foods
I	–	–	–	–	–	–	–	–
II	682	13.53	498	9.88	524	10.40	348	6.91
III	1,224	14.78	842	10.17	986	11.91	628	7.59
IV	1,696	15.36	1,280	11.59	1,326	12.01	1,224	11.09
V	–	–	–	–	–	–	–	–
VI	–	–	–	–	–	–	–	–

Table—4.13 Expenditure Pattern on Different Food Groups as Related to Income Among Muslim Families

Grades	Income level (per annum)	Actual total income	Actual expenditure on foods	Expenditure on foods per cent income	Food Groups			
					I		II	
					Actual expn.	Per cent expn. on foods	Actual expn.	Per cent expn. on foods
I	≤ 5,000	4,080	2,700	66.18	1,380	51.11	488	18.07
II	5,001 – 15,000	9,098	5,662	62.23	2,496	44.08	1,212	21.41
III	15,001 – 25,000	19,763	10,425	52.75	3,722	35.70	2,446	23.46
IV	25,001 – 35,000	29,600	12,000	40,54	3,900	32.50	2,840	23.66
V	35,001 – 45,000	40,650	15,650	38.50	4,585	29.30	3,760	24.03
VI	45,001 +	–	–	–	–	–	–	–

(Contd...)

(Table—4.13 Contd...)

Grades	Food Groups							
	III		IV		V		Other foods	
	Actual expn.	Per cent expn. on foods	Actual expn.	Per cent expn. on foods	Actual expn.	Per cent expn. on foods	Actual expn.	Per cent expn. on foods
I	298	11.03	198	7.33	180	6.66	182	6.74
II	675	11.91	447	7.90	446	7.88	420	7.42
III	1,615	15.49	875	8.39	1,076	10.31	861	8.25
IV	2,120	17.67	1,047	8.72	1,240	10.33	1.020	8.50
V	2,815	17.98	1,475	9.43	1,820	11.63	1,490	9.52
VI	–	–	–	–	–	–	–	–

Table—4.14 Expenditure Pattern on Different Food Groups as Related to Income Among Hindu Families

Grades	Income level (per annum)	Actual total income	Actual expenditure on foods	Expenditure on foods per cent income	Food Groups I		Food Groups II	
					Actual expn.	Per cent expn. on foods	Actual expn.	Per cent expn. on foods
I	≤ 5,000	4,209	2,856	67.84	1,485	51.99	438	15.32
II	5,001 – 15,000	10,212	5,688	55.70	2,283	40.12	915	15.09
III	15,001 – 25,000	19,395	9,216	47.52	2,890	31.36	1,585	17.20
IV	25,001 – 35,000	29,063	12,088	41.59	3,618	29.93	2,097	17.35
V	35,001 – 45,000	38,930	14,859	38.17	4,135	27.83	2,580	17.36
VI	45,001 +	60,792	18,792	30.91	4,853	25.82	3,557	18.93

(Contd...)

(Table—4.14 Contd...)

Grades	Food Groups							
	III		IV		V		Other foods	
	Actual expn.	Per cent expn. on foods	Actual expn.	Per cent expn. on foods	Actual expn.	Per cent expn. on foods	Actual expn.	Per cent expn. on foods
I	338	11.83	211	7.39	182	6.36	225	7.88
II	835	14.69	567	9.79	672	11.81	516	9.09
III	1,493	16.20	977	10.60	1,365	14.82	921	9.99
IV	2,081	17.21	1,234	10.21	1,889	15.63	1,281	10.60
V	2,664	17.93	1,482	9.97	2,300	15.48	1,671	11.25
VI	3,338	17.76	1,826	9.72	2,865	15.25	2,350	12.51

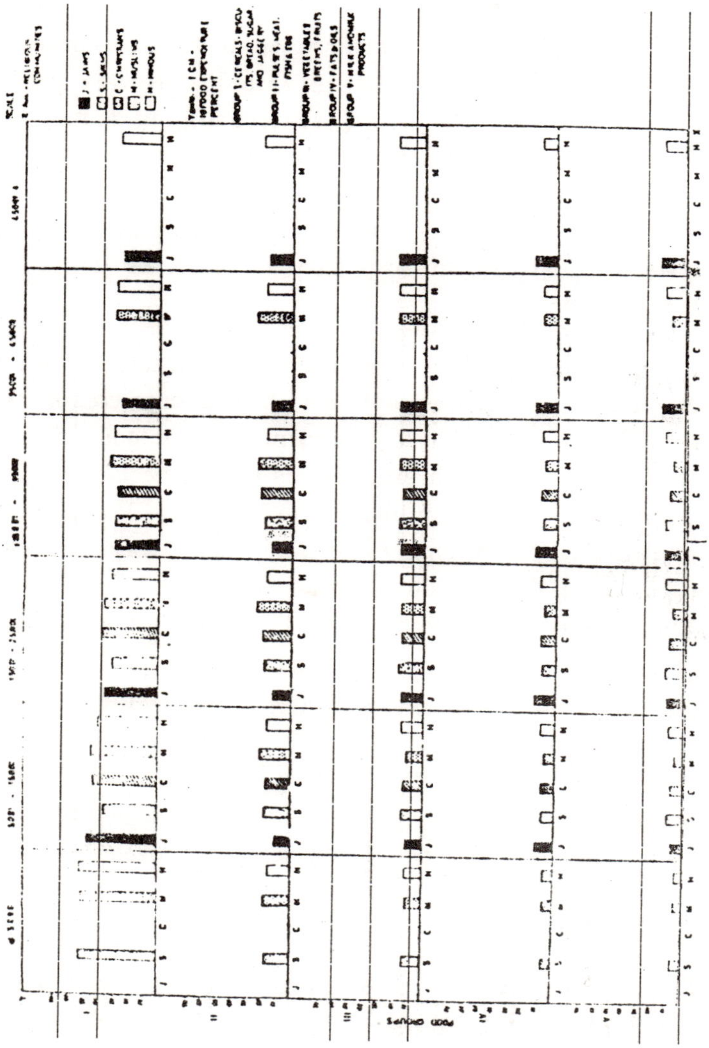

Fig.—4.7 Pattern of Expenditure on the Five Food Groups with Increasing Income Among Different Religious Communities

The food habits of the Sikhs inhabiting Tirupati is somewhat closely related to that of the Hindus. This is probably due to majority of the Sikhs and Hindus living in close proximity for twenty to thirty years. The food practices of both the communities of Sikhs and Hindus are very similar. For example Sikhs in Tirupati are consuming mostly rice unlike their counterparts in North India who generally eat more of wheat. Also in both the communities, there are vegetarians and non-vegetarians. This similarity can be observed in the expenditure pattern of Sikhs and Hindus in all the five food groups.

All the Christians are non-vegetarians. It can be observed that with the exception of the Muslim community, among Christians, the per cent expenditure on foods of group II i.e., pulses, meat, fish and eggs is the highest among the different religious communities. For example, the per cent expenditure on foods among Hindus in food group II ranged from 16.09 in 5,001-15,000 income group to 17.35 in 25,001—35,000 income group. Relatively the Christian community spent 17.70 and 21.85 per cent in grade II and IV respectively on pulses, meat, fish and eggs. Another significant feature is that the increase of per cent expenditure in the food groups other than group I is very small with rising income among Christians, while the decrease in per cent expenditure in group I is substantial.

Like the Christians, all the Muslims surveyed are also non-vegetarians. Hence their per cent expenditure on food group II (pulses, meat, fish and eggs) is the highest among all the religious communities. There is substantial decrease in per cent expenditure on cereals with rising income and the decrease of per cent expenditure from one income group to another group is quite high. The increase of per cent expenditure on various food groups among families belonging to the III, IV and V income groups is not much. The per cent expenditure on food group II for example increased from 23.46 to 23.66 and to 24.03 in III, IV and V income groups respectively. This suggests that after a particular level of income is achieved the increase in per cent expenditure on foods with a further increase in income may not be significant. However the increase in expenditure can be significant when there is initial rise in income.

Among the Hindus also it can be seen that with increasing income, the per cent expenditure on cereals is decreasing and that on other foods is increasing. As in the Muslim community also, the per cent expenditure of the families in food groups II, III, IV and V after the income range of 15,001-25,000 has not increased much. Particularly, the expenditure on group II foods is less when compared to the other religious communities with the exception of Jains. This is because 20 per cent of the Hindus are vegetarians and consequently their expenditure in this group is less.

To sum up, the per cent expenditure of Jains on milk and milk products and vegetables and fruits is highest, which is in accordance with their being lacto-vegetarians. The per cent expenditure of Muslims followed by Christians on food group II (pulses, meat, fish and eggs) is maximum. The expenditure patterns on different foods by Sikhs and Hindus are related as the two communities have been living closely for a long period.

The present survey shows that with an increase in income the expenditure on food group I declines. Though the expenditure on other food groups (II, III, IV and V) is increasing with a use in income, it is high only when the income changed initially. As the income increased further the per cent expenditure on these food groups is small and sometimes is even negligible.

Considering each of the five religious communities, among the Jains, lacto-vegetarianism prevails. As per their religious culture the Jains consume mostly foods of group III and V. Hence the per cent expenditure on these foods is generally higher than that observed among other religious communities at different income levels. For example considering milk and milk products, the per cent expenditure at grade IV income level is 16, 15, 12, 10.3 and 15.6 for Jains, Sikhs, Christians, Muslims and Hindus respectively. Among Muslims and Christians non-vegetarianism prevails and the expenditure on group II foods is high. Among Sikhs and Hindus the expenditure pattern is similar for the different food groups and both vegetarianism and non-vegetarianism prevails.

Choice of Foods and Nutritional Patterns Among Different Religious Communities

Nutritionists have stated that if all the basic five foods are included in the daily diet in adequate amounts then the nutrient needs of the human body can be well met. The basic five food items contain all the nutrients that are essential for health. In the light of these observations, one of the objective of this study was to survey and study the food choices and nutritional patterns of different religious communities.

To facilitate systematic and scientific analysis, generally, the food choices are studied on the basis of division of foods into basic five:

I—Cereals, bread, sugar and jaggery

II—Pulses and fleshy foods

III—Vegetables and fruits

IV—Fats and oils

V—Milk and milk products.

The information obtained has been analysed on the basis of the above foods consumed per day in a regular, irregular and occasional manner among families of different religious communities.

When the families consumed items from each of the five food groups daily and consistently, they are classified under regular. If the families consumed all the basic five food items in a day twice or thrice a week but not consistently, they are classified under irregular. In the group termed as occasional, the families are consuming one or more of the basic five food items daily, only once in a fortnight or even at longer intervals.

From the information given in Table—4.15, it can be seen that out of 650 families surveyed 69 per cent of them are in the regular group. Twenty four per cent of the families are in the irregular group, while 7 per cent of them are in the occasional group.

Table—4.15 Per cent Distribution of Families of Different Religious Communities as per the Frequency of Choice of Foods of all Five Groups in a Day

Religion	Number of families	Frequency of choice of basic five foods		
		Regular	Irregular	Occasional
Jain	10	90.00 (9)	10.00 (1)	—
Sikh	20	75.00 (15)	15.00 (3)	10.00 (2)
Christian	20	85.00 (17)	10.00 (2)	5.00 (1)
Muslim	100	65.00 (65)	24.00 (24)	11.00 (11)
Hindu	500	68.60 (343)	25.60 (128)	5.80 (29)
Total	**650**	**69.08 (449)**	**24.31 (158)**	**6.62 (43)**

Table—4.16 Distribution of Families of Different Religious Communities as per the Choice of Foods of each of the Basic Five Groups in a Day

Food groups	Frequency of choice of different foods		
	Regular	Irregular	Occasional
(1)	(2)	(3)	(4)
Jains:			
Group I	100.00 (10)	–	–
II	100.00 (10)	–	–
III	90.00 (9)	10.00 (1)	–
IV	100.00 (10)	–	–
V	100.00 (10)	–	–
Sikhs:			
Group I	100.00 (20)	–	–
II	90.00 (18)	10.00 (2)	–
III	90.00 (18)	10.00 (2)	–
IV	100.00 (20)	–	–
V	95.00 (19)	5.00 (1)	–
Christians:			
Group I	100.00 (20)	–	–
II	95.00 (19)	5.00 (1)	–
III	95.00 (19)	5.00 (1)	–
IV	100.00 (20)	–	–
V	95.00 (19)	5.00 (1)	–

(1)		(2)	(3)	(4)
Muslims:				
	Group I	100.00 (100)	–	–
	II	72.00 (72)	24.00 (24)	4.00 (4)
	III	65.00 (65)	30.00 (30)	5.00 (5)
	IV	100.00 (100)	–	–
	V	89.00 (89)	7.00 (7)	4.00 (4)
Hindus:				
	Group I	100.00 (500)	–	–
	II	68.60 (343)	26.40 (132)	5.00 (25)
	III	82.40 (412)	15.40 (77)	2.20 (11)
	IV	100.00 (500)	–	–
	V	90.60 (453)	5.80 (29)	3.60 (18)

Table—4.16 shows that in all the religious communities except that of the Jains, the families under the irregular group are missing in food items in groups II, III and V *i.e.,* pulses and fleshy foods, vegetables and fruits and milk and milk products. It is only among the Muslim and Hindu communities that a few families of occasional group are not choosing foods from groups II, III and V. In each religious community, majority of the families belonging to higher income groups are consuming the basic five food items regularly. But the dietary pattern of the families in the lower income group of all the religious communities indicates that their diet is deficient in one or more food items of the basic five. These low income groups come under irregular and occasional group classification. Irrespective of income groups all families are choosing cereals (group I) and fats and oils (group IV) regularly.

Considering each of the five religious communities, the food consumption pattern of the Jains is far better compared to that of the families belonging to the other religious communities. Out of the ten families observed nine of them belong to the regular group, while only one family belongs to the irregular group. The one family which has an irregular pattern is not consuming vegetables regularly which belong to group III of the basic five food group (Ref. Table—4.16). The Jains are essentially lacto-vegetarians, and fruits should have an important place in their menu plan. However, the choice of vegetables and fruits is limited. They are choosing costly vegetables like cabbage, cauliflower, carrot, potato etc. Green leafy vegetables are consumed rarely among Jains though their diet is essentially vegetarian. Regarding the one family which is in the irregular group, the consumption of costly items of vegetables is at long intervals. Even greens which are cheap are not consumed regularly. This indicates that all the Jain families generally are not in the habit of choosing green leafy vegetables. The income range of the Jain family which belongs to the irregular group is 5,001—15,000. There is one other family among Jains which belongs to the same income range (Ref. Table—4.8). However, this family is able to consume all the basic five foods regularly probably because of its small family size. The family under irregular group which is not consuming basic III food items consistently has a large family size. The total number of members of the family in irregular group is seven as against three for the family belonging to the regular group, the income range being the same for the two families. The large family size may be partly responsible for the limited choice of food items from group III. This is so inspite of the expenditure on food (Rs. 6,600 per annum) being about the same for both families. This indicates that this one Jain family is not in the habit of choosing vegetables regularly apart from the large family size affecting the choice.

The large family size warrants large quantities of vegetables, which are very expensive in Tirupati. Therefore the vegetables are out of reach of the family for daily consumption. These families, tend to rely more on pulses which are relatively cheaper. Also on an overall basis, the consumption of greens by all the Jain families is limited.

Among the Sikhs, 75 per cent of the families belong to the regular group. Other 25 per cent of the families are not consuming pulses and fleshy foods, vegetables and fruits and milk and milk products (Groups II, III and V) regularly (Ref. Table—4.16). These families of the irregular group are consuming the above stated food items only for special occasions and festivals or when they have additional income from profits. The Sikh families under irregular group belong to miscellaneous occupations such as coffee and snack vendors, fruit sellers, cloth merchants, retail basket sellers, taxi driver etc. The income of these families ranges between Rs. 4,000-8,000 per annum. The income of all these families is highly irregular, depending on the fluctuating demands of the consumer. As a result, these families consume foods of all the basic five food groups when they earn a high income and refrain from certain food items when their income is normal or sometimes even low.

In the Christian community out of twenty, seventeen families are in the regular group which is relatively better compared to the other religious communities with the exception of Jains. The other three families (15%) belong to the irregular group. Among these three families one is missing basic II (pulses and fleshy foods) the other basic III (vegetables and fruits) and the third basic V (milk and milk products). This may be due to the low economic status of these families. All the Christian families are non-vegetarians. Compared to the Muslim community, which is also non-vegetarian, 85 per cent of the Christian families are in the regular group while only 65 per cent of the Muslim families are in the regular group.

Considering the case of Muslim community, out of a hundred families surveyed, 65 of them are in regular group. 24 in the irregular group with another 11 in the occasional group. The families in the regular group are not consuming pulses regularly but are taking more of low quality non-vegetarian food items such as legs and wings of chicken, mutton bones, dry fish and beef. It is in the Muslim community that more number of families are missing food items from groups II, III and V relative to all other religious communities. Thirty per cent of the families are not consuming vegetable and fruits regularly. Also the consumption of costly vegetables such as beans, cabbage, cauliflower etc., is less. Relatively cheaper vegetables such as greens, cluster beans, ladies finger etc., are consumed more by Muslims. Some families (7%) are also not taking milk and milk products regularly. These families are not consuming curds but are generally using butter milk. They buy milk only on festivals and special occasions to prepare kheer and other milk preparations.

Among the Hindu families sixty nine per cent of them are consuming regularly foods from the 5 food groups, a quarter of them are in the irregular group, while 6 per cent of them are in occasional group. It is observed that a large per cent of the Hindus, who are non-vegetarians are not consuming fleshy foods regularly and are doing so only when they can afford to or have additional income from profits. Many of the lower income families are using chutneys rather than curry preparations with vegetables. Some of them cannot afford even chutneys and depend on pickles as a side dish. Also 4 per cent of low income groups are not consuming any milk and milk products. Many families are in the habit of taking tea early in the morning. They buy it from the vendor who makes regular rounds as they feel that buying milk is beyond their means.

Among all the five religious communities, it is the Jains, Sikhs and Christians who are consuming a better planned diet relative to the others. This may be due to the better economic status of the Jains and a higher educational and occupational status of the Sikh and Christian communities. It is among the Muslim and Hindu communities that a large per cent of the families are illiterates and have low occupational and economic status. As a result of these factors a 30-35 per cent of the families fall among the irregular and occasional groups.

From Tables—4.15 and 4.16, it can be observed that income is playing a dominant role in the consumption pattern of foods of different groups among the different religious communities. It is the relatively poor families that are not able to choose all the essential food items. This clearly proves the direct relationship between income and food expenditure pattern. Other factors which influence choice of foods from the different food groups are religion and habits. The Jains for example are not consume meat and fleshy foods as per religious regulation and they do not consume leafy vegetables by habit.

A Study of Combination of Foods through Menu Patterns Among Different Religious Communities

In the previous sections the discussion on the food expenditure pattern and the choice of foods give an indication of limitation in the choice of foods and frequency of consumption of foods apart from the amount spent on different foods from the income of the families of differing socio-economic levels. However, these patterns do not indicate the actual combinations of foods in recipes practised by different religious communities. A study of the general menu pattern of the recipes listed for the different meals in a day gives the information on the various combinations of the foods.

In this context, *Ritchie (1967)* emphasized the importance of studying the general menu patterns. He stated that information on meal pattern gives an indication of the easiest possible way to improve the nutritional intake of the various groups.

In the light of the importance given to studying the general menu patterns, information related to menu pattern has been organised as per the three groups regular, irregular, occasional among the different religious communities.

In Tables—4.17 and 4.18 the menu items have been classified for breakfast, lunch, tea and dinner. For each meal all the recipes which are generally prepared are listed. In Table—4.17 the menu items consumed by the Jains have been presented while in Table—4.18, the menu items consumed by the other four religious communities—Sikh, Christian, Muslim and Hindu have been presented together.

People belonging to same socio-economic status irrespective of religion have been living in close proximity for a long time. Hence the items they chose and prepare are similar though the families belong to different religious communities. To some extent the availability of foods in a particular locality and their cost have a bearing on the type of preparations practised among these communities. On the other hand the Jains belong to a higher socio-economic status and they live separately as a congregation in the business centre of Tirupati. This type of living and their higher socio-economic status allows them to follow nutritional practices which are different from those of the other religious communities. Their preparations are purely vegetarian as dictated by their religion. Some of their menu items are exclusive, for example, Greengram kootu, Bengal gram fry and Pacchi Kootu.

However, this does not mean that only Jains are influenced by religion. All the communities are influenced by their religions, but they are not in a position to strictly adhere to their religious recommendations or restrictions on

Table—4.17 Common Menu Items per day for the Regular and Irregular Groups Among the Jain Community

	Regular	Irregular
Breakfast		
	Bread and Jam/Sooca Rotti with subji (bengalgram + greengram)/Idli with Sambar/Dosa with Chutney/Vada with Sambar	Idli with Sambar/Vada with Sambar/Dosa with Chutney/Sooca Rotti with subji (bengalgram + greengram) Bread with Jam.
	Note: Any one item is selected from the above breakfast items. Coffee/Milk.	**Note:** Any one item is selected from the above breakfast items. Coffee/Milk.
Lunch		
	Cereal preparation:	*Cereal preparation:*
	Chapati Rice	Chapati Rice
	Pulse preparation:	*Pulse preparation:*
	Dhal sambar/Pesala Kootu/Senagu Kootu/Bengalgram fry/Peas curry.	Dhal sambar/Greengram Kootu/ Bengalgram fry/Peas curry.
	Vegetable preparations:	*Vegetable preparations:*
	Vegetable curry (Beans, Cabbage, Cauliflower, Carrot)/Ladies finger fry/Tomato curry/Pumpkin curry/Potato curry/Pacchi Kootu (Mango, Ladies finger, Pumpkin, Keru and Kummateru)	Ladies finger fry/Tomato curry/Pumpkin curry/Potato curry/Pacchi Kootu (Mango, Ladies finger, Pumpkin, Keru and Kummateru)/Beans fry.

(Contd...)

(Table—4.17 Contd...)

	Regular	Irregular
	Pickles and Chutney preparations: Coconut Chutney/Bengalgram Chutney/Groundnut Chutney/Mango Pickles/Lemon Pickle.	*Pickles and Chutney preparations:* Groundnut Chutney/Coconut Chutney/Bengalgram Chutney/Mango Pickle/Lemon Pickle.
	Note: From the above preparations any one item is selected for Lunch	*Note:* From the above preparations any one item is selected for Lunch
	Dhal rasam/Tomato rasam/Curds/Butter Milk.	Dhal rasam/Tomato rasam/Butter Milk.
	Fruits: Banana/Apple/Sweet lime/Grapes	*Fruits:* Banana/Grapes Note: Weekly once or twice.
Snacks	*Sweets:* Powdered Bengalgram Laddu/Palakova/Basundi/Badam milk/Mysore pak/Groundnut Chikkies/Gulab Jamun/Rasagulla/Jangiri/Ice cream.	*Sweets:* Laddu/Gulab Jamun/Mysore pak/Basundi/Palakova/Rasagulla/Groundnut Chikkies
	Savories:	*Savories:*
	Pakodi/Bajji/Bonda/Mixture/Muruku *Note:* Any one from the above preparations. Coffee/milk/tea.	Pakodi/Bonda/Mixture/Muruku *Note:* Any one from the above preparations. Coffee/tea.
Dinner	Pulka	Pulka
	Note: Same items as those consumed at lunch time.	*Note:* Same items as those consumed at lunch time.
10.00 p.m.	Milk	Milk

Table—4.18 Common Menu Items per day for the Regular, Irregular and Occasional Groups Among, Sikh, Christian, Muslim and Hindu Communities

	Regular	Irregular	Occasional
Breakfast	Idli/Upma/Puri/Chapati/ Dosa/Lemon Rice/Vada/ Pasarattu/Pongali	Idli/Upma/Dosa/Pongali/ Leomon Rice/Chapati/Puri/ Vada/Pasarattu	Idli with Chutney/ Dosa with Chutney/ Upma/Pongali/Vada
	Non-vegetarian:		
	Bread and omlet Pickles/Chutney that are used for breakfast:	Pickles/Chutneys that are used for breakfast:	Rice + Pickle Coffee/Tea
	Groundnut Chutney/Bombai Chutney/Coconut Chutney/ Ginger Chutney/Tomato with Onion Chutney/Mango (or) Lemon Pickles	Groundnut Chutney/Coconut Chutney/Tomato Chutney/ Mango Pickle/Lemon Pickle	
		Coffee	
	Note: Any one item selected from the above breakfast items		
	Coffee		

(Contd...)

(Table—4.18 Contd...)

	Regular	Irregular	Occasional
Lunch	*Cereal preparation:*	*Cereal preparation:*	*Cereal preparation:*
	Rice/Chapati/Sangati	Rice/Sangati	Rice/Sangati
	Note: Sometimes Sikh community selected chapati as their lunch item.		
	Pulse preparation	*Pulse preparation*	*Pulse preparation*
	Dhal sambar/Dhal sambar with either brinjal (or) greens (or) beens (or) drumstic (or) vegetables Bengalgram dhal sambar.	Dhal sambar/Dhal sambar with either greens (or) drumstic (or) brinjal (or) vegetables	Dhal sambar/Dhal sambar with greens or brinjal (or) drumstics
	Vegetable preparation	*Vegetable preparation*	*Vegetable preparation*
	Curry preparation:	*Curry preparation:*	*Curry preparation:*
	Brinjal/Beans/Cabbage/ Tomato/Drumstic/Greens/ Peas/Culiflower/Ladies finger/ Beet root/Pumpkin/Potato	Brinjal/Cabbage/Tomato Greens/Drumstic/Beans Ladies finger/Cluster beans/Potato/Peas	Brinjal curry/Greens curry/Beans curry/ Tomato curry/Cabbage curry/Potato curry

(Contd...)

(Table—4.18 Contd...)

Regular	Irregular	Occasional
Fried preparation:	*Fried preparation:*	*Fried preparation:*
Brinjal/Beans/Cabbage/Dondakai/Colacasia/Potato/Yam/Carrot/Drumstic/Cluster beans/Potato+Brinjal/Beans + Carrot.	Brinjal/Cabbage/Drumstic/Potato/Colacasia/Beans/Dondakai/Cucumbar/Carrot Beetroot/Beans + carrot.	Ladies finger fry/Cluster beans fry
Fleshy food preparation:	*Fleshy food preparation:*	*Fleshy food preparation:*
Mutton curry (or) fry Chicken curry (or) fry Fish curry (or) fry Egg curry (or) fry	Mutton curry/Chicken curry/Fish curry/ Egg fry/curry	Mutton curry/Dry fish fry/Egg fry
Chutney preparation:	*Chutney preparation:*	*Chutney preparation:*
Gongura/Coconut/Tomato/Pudeena/Corriander/Blackgram/Redgram	Redgram/Blackgram/Gongura/Pudeena/Coconut/Corriander/Tomato	Redgram/Blackgram/Tomato/Gongura/Pudeena/Corriander
Pickles preparation:	*Pickles preparation:*	*Pickles preparation:*
Mango/Lemon/Tomato/Tamarind/Drumstic/Amla	Mango/Lemon/Tomato	Mango/Lemon

(Contd...)

(Table—4.18 Contd...)

Regular	Irregular	Occasional
Other Items:	*Other Items:*	*Other Items:*
Papads/Vadiyalu/Dry Chillies/Pumpkin Vadiyalu/Orugulu	Pappads/Vadiyalu/ Orugulu	Pappads
Note: From the above preparations any one item selected	*Note:* From the above preparations either vegetables (or) pulse (or) fleshy foods (or) chutney item is selected	*Note:* From the above preparations any one item is selected.
Dhal Rasam/Tomato Rasam/ Pepper Rasam	Dhal Rasam/Pepper Rasam/ Tomato Rasam	Dhal Rasam/Pepper Rasam/
Curds/Butter milk	Butter milk	Butter milk Note: Once (or) twice a week
Fruits:	*Fruits:*	*Fruits:*
Banana/Apple/ Sweet lime/Grapes	Banana/Grapes *Note:* Weekly once on twice	–

(*Contd...*)

(Table—4.18 Contd...)

	Regular	Irregular	Occasional
Snacks	*Sweets:*	*Sweets:*	*Sweets:*
	Arisalu/Groundnut/ Chikkies/Puffed Rice laddu/Kesari/Gulab Jamun/ Laddu/Mysore Pak/Biscuits Ice cream/Custard/ Fruit salad.	Groundnut Chikkies/ Puffed Rice Laddu/ Kesari/Arisalu/Gulabjam/ Mysore Pak/Biscuits/ Custard.	Chikkies/Biscuits/ Arisalu/Murukulu/ Laddu
	Savories:	***Savories:***	***Savories:***
	Bajji/Bonda/Pakoda/ Samosa/Murukulu/ Karapupak/Mixture	Murukulu/Karapu poosa/ Bajji/Bonda/Pakoda Mixture	— — —
	Note: Any one from the above preparation	*Note:* Any one from the above preparation	
	Coffee/Tea.	Coffee/Tea.	Coffee/Tea.
Dinner	Pulka Chapati	Pulka Chapati	
	Note: 1. Few families selected the above cereal items. 2. Same items as those consumed at Lunch time	*Note:* 1. Few families selected the above cereal item 2. Same items as those consumed at Lunch time.	*Note:* Same items as those consumed at Lunch time.

* *Only Muslim and Hindu families are in occasional group.*

** *The underlined items are consumed daily*

foods due to the significant impact of other factors like social and economic status. While all the Jains are doing business, irrespective of their educational status, the members of all the other four religious communities are engaged in various occupations depending upon their educational status. The members of these four communities also have good social relations, while the members of the Jain community remain apart. Women belonging to the Jain community do not mix with other communities. Some of the reasons may be heavy work load, a result of joint family system and language problem. While in the case of the other four communities differing occupational status and social relations are influencing the menu pattern minimum social relations, exclusive occupation and better economic status may have more impact on the Jains strict adherence to religious recommendations on food consumption. However, all the communities observe religious recommendation on food during special occasions, festivals and other religious functions, when they spend more money disregarding their economic status.

The menu plan of the Jain Community shows that their food preparations largely consist of wheat (Chapati, Pulka, Poori etc.) pulses (Sambar, Kootu, Fries, Curries etc.) milk (Palakova, Basundi, Badam milk etc.) and to a lesser extent rice (Idli or Dosa) and vegetables (Vegetable Curry, Tomato Curry etc.). Their menu is exclusive in that there is total absence of food preparations using root vegetables and leafy vegetables.

The common menu plan of the four religious groups (Sikh, Christian, Muslim and Hindu) shows that their food preparations are different from that of the Jain community. Their food preparations are mostly products of rice (Idli, Dosa, Lime Rice, Pongali, etc). vegetables (Brinjal and Beans Curry, Ladies Finger, Cluster Beans Fry etc.), of root vegetables (Potato Curry, Colocasia Fry, Yam Curry etc.), of non-vegetarian foods (Chicken Curry, Mutton Fry, Egg Curry etc.), and to a lesser extent of pulses (Sambar with Vegetables) and wheat (Puri and Chapati).

The daily menu of the Jains is characterised by wheat, pulse and milk preparations while that of the other communities, largely consists of rice, vegetable and non-vegetarian preparations. Only some families in the Sikh and Hindu religious communities consume non-vegetarian preparations. The menu plan of the Jains show the influence of their religion on food, while that of the other religious communities shows the greater influence of socio-economic factors.

Food Pattern During Festivals Among Different Religious Communities

In almost every religion, festivals make an important contribution to diets. Statements of one type or another pertaining to man's diet can be found in the sacred books and writings. As these dietary regulations were actually written down in the sacred books, which were often considered the word or will of the supreme being, the regulations have been preserved and perpetuated over the centuries. Religion itself has encouraged and contributed to the continuing observance of these dietary habits from earlier times. The present survey also shows that among all the five religious communities surveyed all the families celebrate festivals by preparing special and additional foods irrespective of their economic status. All of them insist on consuming special dishes on festival days. Some of the special dishes prepared are as follows:

From Table—4.19, it may be observed that Jain families consume sweets prepared with ghee, refined wheat flour, milk and coconuts for all their festivals. Sweet preparations predominate on festival occasions. They are strict vegetarians. Sikhs also consume vegetarian foods during festival days though at other times, some of them consume non-vegetarian items. Sweets such as Jangri, Laddu, Payasam and Poleelu, hot preparations such as Vadai, Mixture, are also prepared.

Table—4.19 Food Preparations During Festivals Among Different Religious Communities

Religion and Festivals	Time of the year	Food Preparations
(1)	(2)	(3)
Jainism		
Holi	March	Khajapuri, Burfi, Gujiya, Gulabjam
Deepavali	October/ November	Coconut Burfi, Kova
Rakhee	May	Chakkilalu, Mysore pak
Dasara	October	Lapse, Pakodi
Peryusam	August	Fasting (Hot water) for one day
Sikkhism		
Holi	March	Vada, Jangri, Mixture
Deepavali	October/ November	Laddu, Puri
Sri Ram Navami	April	Laddu, Poleelu, Vadapappu
Rakhee	May	Vadai, Payasam
Gurunanak Birthday	October	Sugeelu, Vadai
Christianity		
Christmas	December	Cakes, Rose Cakes, Doughnuts, Muruku, Kajji Kayalu, Mixture
New Year's day	January	Mutton Biryani, Chicken Fry (or) Curry
Good Friday	April	Arisalu, Payasam, Vadai.
Easter	April	Arisalu, Payasam, Vadai

(Contd...)

Islam		
Ramjan	March/April	Fasting for 40 days prior of festival Vermicelli Payasam, Biryani, Meat Curry, Brinjal Curry, Sweet (any)
Bakrid	September	Chapati, Mutton Biryani, Sweet (any)
Muharram	October	Sharbath (Sugar+Milk), Biryani, Meat curry, Sweet (any)
Hinduism		
Bhoji and Kanuma	January	Dosai (or) Idli, Mutton
Sankranti	January	Vadai, Payasam, Laddu, Chakkarapongali
Ugadhi	April	Ugadhi Pacchadi, Vadai, Sugeelu (or) Poleelu
Vinayaka Chavithi	September	Vadai, Payasam, Kudumulu, Undralu
Deepavali	October/ November	Arisalu, Sugeelu, Pulihora, Potato Curry, Vadai
Dasara	October	Vadai, Payasam, Pulihora, Arisalu, Sugeelu
Gamgamma Jathara (Local festival)	May	Dosai (or) Idli, Mutton,
Varalakshmi Vratham Sreeramanavami and Sivarathri	August April February	Vadapappu, Vadai, Payasam, Sundal

Christians and Muslims use fleshy foods and eggs in various preparations and non-vegetarianism is practised for all the festivals. Special rice preparation such as mutton biryani, biryani and sweets such as cakes, payasam, arisalu, sharbath are common for both Christians and Muslims.

Among the Hindus, a variety of vegetarian dishes are consumed on most of the festival days. However, non-vegetarian dishes are consumed rarely on festivals such as Bhogi, Kanuma and Gangamma Jatara. Eventhough Bhogi, Sankranti and Kanuma are three days of the Harvest festival of Hindus, non-vegetarian foods may be consumed on Bhogi and Kanuma, but on Sankranti purely vegetarian foods may be eaten. On Naraka-chathurdashi, first day of Deepavali festival, non-vegetarian foods are consumed by some families. However, these families consume only vegetarian foods on Deepavali. Cereal preparations such as Dosa, Idli and Arisalu, pulse preparations such as Vada, Poleelu, Sugeelu etc., are common for a number of festivals during the year.

It can be concluded that, in contrast to their daily life, all families among the different religions are preparing and consuming a variety of rich foods without considering the income or budget restraints. In fact festival expenditure occupies an important place in the budget of every family. This in itself indicates the significant influence or religious festivals on food habits. The special dishes that are prepared on festival days are in addition to the regular items consumed. In this way the special dishes can contribute to a certain extent to improve the nutritional status of the families.

Methods of Preservation Practices Among Different Religious Communities

In any study of nutritional practices, information on preservation of foods is important as preservation prevents wastage of foods in season and permits use of certain foods during all seasons of the year. This information is also necessary to bring about changes if any in the preservation techniques currently followed, to promote better methods of preservation and to introduce newer methods.

The information in Table—4.20 gives the extent to which the families are practising or not practising preservation and the per cent of families following the different methods of preservation.

Majority of the families in all the religious communities are preserving foods while all the Jain families are preserving foods. Among Sikhs and Christians, 90 per cent of the families are preserving foods. About 75 per cent of the Muslim and Hindu families are also preserving foods.

With regard to the different methods of preservation the majority of the families are preserving foods by the pickling method in all religious groups. With the exception of the Christians about 30 per cent of the families in all the other religious communities are preserving foods by dehydration. The Christians are practising dehydration to a greater extent that is 50 per cent of the families surveyed. It is observed that among the Christian families, Vadiyalu are being prepared out of rice and sago by the dehydration process to a greater extent than among families of other religions. This accounts for the difference observed in the extent of practice of dehydration between Christian and other communities.

When compared to the other religious communities, majority of the Hindus are following pickling and dehydrating methods for mangoes and lime for their consumption throughout the year. A large per cent of the Hindus (54%) belong to the lower and lower middle income group. They are not able to afford expensive vegetables for daily consumption. Hence they buy mangoes and lime seasonally at cheap rates and preserve them.

Table—4.20 Preservation Methods Prevalent Among Different Religious Communities

Religion	Practising Preservation		Method of Preservation			
	Yes	No	Pickling	Dehydration	Pickling and Dehydration	Sugar Concentration
Jain	100.00 (10)	–	100.00 (10)	30.00 (3)	40.00 (4)	60.00 (6)
Sikh	90.00 (18)	10.00 (2)	90.00 (18)	30.00 (6)	20.00 (4)	40.00 (8)
Christian	90.00 (18)	10.00 (2)	90.00 (18)	50.00 (10)	30.00 (6)	35.00 (7)
Muslim	76.00 (76)	24.00 (24)	76.00 (76)	34.00 (34)	35.00 (35)	22.00 (22)
Hindu	75.20 (376)	24.80 (124)	75.20 (376)	29.00 (145)	44.00 (220)	29.60 (148)

Sugar concentration method was practised to the greatest extent by Jains (60%). This method requires more money and fuel. It may be observed that most of the Jains belong to the higher income group and consequently are able to resort to the more expensive form of preserving foods. Moreover they prefer sweets to savouries for all occasions.

Considering the religious communities, separately among the Jains, pickling is used to the maximum degree, while dehydration is the least practiced. Sixty per cent of the Jain families are preserving fruits like tomato, mangoes and limes.

Among the Sikh families also, 90 per cent of them preserve foods in the form of pickles. A small per cent of them resort to dehydration as well as pickling and dehydration (20-30%), 40 per cent of them make jams and squashes. Compared to all other methods a higher per cent of the families prepare pickles, jams and squashes.

A similar trend may be noticed among the Christian community also except in the case of dehydration process which is practiced by 50 per cent of the families.

A higher per cent (75%) of the Muslim and Hindu families also make pickles while 25-25 per cent preserve foods by dehydration pickling and dehydration. A small per cent (22-29%) also make jams and squashes.

On the whole it may be stated that a higher per cent of the Jains follow pickling and sugar concentration, while more number of Christian families follow dehydration and Hindus are preserving foods both by pickling and dehydration.

Irrespective of their religion, many of the families belonging to lower income groups consider pickles and other preserved food as a main dish and served it in place of curry. On the other hand the higher income groups consider preserved foods either as a delicacy or a variety food or an additional dish. Among the middle income group, preservation is done as preserved foods would be useful in the case of an emergency or could be used as an extra item, when there were sudden visitors or when they are short of money. Thus the attitude of the families to preserving foods among all the religious groups differs. These different attitudes ate mainly due to differences in income.

Foods are generally prepared and preserved seasonally when they are available in large quantities at cheap rates. In all the religious communities, the foods that are generally preserved by pickling are mangoes, lime, tomatoes, drumsticks and amla, pappads, vadiyalu and pickled chillies are the items prepared with rice and blackgram, rice and sago, and chillies respectively. The chillies are dried after they are soaked in salt and butter milk. All the various items prepared under pickles and dry preservatives are salted.

These food items are prepared once a year, generally in summer. Usually the pickling and dehydration method is undertaken by lower, and lower middle income groups, as it does not require expensive ingredients like oil. Generally mangoes and lime are cut, mixed with salt and chilly powder and then dried. In addition sweetened preservatives like tomatoes, mangoes, limes etc., are prepared in the form of jams and squashes. Squashes are prepared in summer, while Jams are prepared seasonally, when vegetables and fruits are available at cheap rates.

Method of Preparation and Cooking Practices Among Different Religious Communities

Nutritional practices though generally originate by historical accident are interwoven with emotional and cultural life of the people. They are passed on from generation to generation by the social training given to the young. Economic considerations also largely influence food habits and their choice. In addition to the availability of food, families become used to specific foods only because those particular foods are within their purchasing power. Further any study on food habits should also cover food preparation and cooking methods followed by different groups. Such information can form the basis for educating the target groups to bring about viable changes in cooking practices and prevent the loss of nutrients.

Mead and Guthe (1943) and *Richie (1962)* stated that information on various methods of preparation and cooking of foods is important in studying the factors influencing food habits. Table—4.21 presents the percentage distribution of families according to the methods of preparation and cooking of different foods among different religious communities.

Considering the straining method of cooking rice, the Jains do not use this method at all, while 78 per cent of the Muslim families are following it. The lowest number of families following this practice are among Christians. Of the total number of families surveyed 45 per cent of the Sikh and 59 per cent of Hindus are using straining for cooking rice. The conjee that is obtained from straining is more often thrown away than consumed. Among the Muslims, almost 81 per cent of the families throwaway the cooking water, while 19 per cent of the them consume the rice conjee. The Christian families do not consume the rice conjee at all, while 44 per cent of the Sikhs 'consume the conjee and 56 per cent throw it away. Majority of the Hindu families practising the straining method of cooking rice throw away the rice conjee.

The two methods of cooking rice—non-straining and pressure cooking prevent the loss of nutrients and are practised by most of the Jains followed by Christians and Sikhs, only a small percentage of Muslims are following these practices. Eleven per cent of these families are practising non-straining and pressure cooking for rice. Among the Hindus 27 per cent of the families have adopted the pressure cooking and 14 per cent the non-straining method. Considering the pressure cooking method, a large number of Christian families follow the method, while the Sikhs and Hindus take the second and third place respectively. It can

Table—4.21 A Comparison of Methods of Preparation and Cooking of Foods Among Different Religious Communities

Religion	Method of cooking Rice			Use of Rice Conjee		Choice of Rice			
	Straining	Non-straining	Pressure cooking	Consumed	Throw-away	Par-boiled rice	Highly polished rice	Moderately polished rice	Home pounded
Jain	–	80.00 (8)	20.00 (2)	–	–	–	90.00 (9)	10.00 (1)	–
Sikh	45.00 (9)	25.00 (5)	30.00 (6)	44.44 (4)	55.56 (5)	–	65.00 (13)	35.00 (7)	–
Christian	25.00 (5)	25.00 (5)	50.00 (10)	–	100.00 (5)	–	90.00 (18)	10.00 (2)	–
Muslims	78.00 (78)	11.00 (11)	11.00 (11)	19.23 (15)	80.77 (63)	2.00 (2)	64.00 (64)	32.00 (32)	2.00 (2)
Hindu	59.10 (296)	14.20 (71)	26.60 (133)	15.88 (47)	84.12 (249)	5.60 (28)	65.20 (326)	20.40 (102)	8.80 (44)

(Contd...)

(Table—4.21 Contd...)

Religion	Cooking method for pulses		Cooking method for vegetables				Preparation of vegetables for cooking		Amount of water used for vegetables in cooking	
	Boiling	Pressure cooking	Boiling	Steaming	Boiling and Frying	Frying	Cut and wash	Wash and cut	Excess and throw-away	Suffi-cient
Jain	30.00 (3)	70.00 (7)	20.00 (2)	50.00 (5)	90.00 (9)	100.00 (10)	40.00 (4)	60.00 (6)	40.00 (4)	60.00 (6)
Sikh	65.00 (13)	35.00 (7)	5.00 (1)	60.00 (12)	95.00 (19)	80.00 (16)	45.00 (9)	55.00 (11)	40.00 (8)	60.00 (12)
Christian	45.00 (9)	55.00 (11)	40.00 (8)	60.00 (12)	95.00 (19)	95.00 (19)	40.00 (8)	60.00 (12)	35.00 (7)	65.00 (13)
Muslims	88.00 (88)	12.00 (12)	6.00 (6)	15.00 (15)	94.00 (94)	78.00 (78)	73.00 (73)	27.00 (27)	64.00 (64)	36.00 (36)
Hindu	69.00 (345)	31.00 (155)	36.40 (182)	29.00 (145)	98.20 (491)	91.40 (457)	43.20 (216)	56.80 (284)	33.00 (165)	67.00 (335)

be observed that Jains are following relatively modern methods of cooking, while the Muslims tend to use traditional methods which lead to loss of nutrients.

In general it is observed that almost all the families irrespective of religion use highly polished rice. The reason given is that highly polished rice is clean and tasty. Some respondents stated that they buy polished rice as they have enough money to do so. They feel that parboiled rice is mostly consumed by people who cannot afford highly polished rice. This indicates that respondents belonging to higher economic status are giving more importance to the prestige factor. They feel that certain foods are to be consumed only by the low income group even though they may be nutritious foods. This finding is in agreement with that of Moore (1952) who found out that American foods become hoity-toity, if they are rare, expensive, exceptionally difficult to prepare or frequently liked or extreme in favour of taste qualities. Ten per cent of the Jains and Christians consume moderately polished rice as against a large percentage (90%) consuming highly polished rice. More than thirty per cent of the Sikh and Muslims are also consuming moderately polished rice. Twenty per cent of Hindu families are also consuming moderately polished rice. The Christians and the Jains are on par with regard to the choice of highly polished rice and moderately polished rice. However, in all the communities the percentage of people consuming moderately polished rice was low compared to the consumption of highly polished rice. This difference can be seen more among the Jains and Christians especially. A few families belonging to Muslim and Hindu communities consume parboiled rice. This is not due to their nutritional knowledge but because they feel that parboiled rice fills their stomach and they are not hungry for a long period of time. They also acknowledge that parboiled rice is comparatively cheaper and healthier, while milled rice causes joint pains. None of the Jain, Sikh and Christian families used home pounded rice, while very few families among Muslims and Hindus consumed home pounded rice.

With regard to the cooking of pulses, most of the families (65-88%) in Sikh, Muslim and Hindu communities are using boiling method. But in the case of Jains and Christians mostly they use pressure cooker (55-70%). Even while cooking of rice, these two communities mostly use pressure cooker. Among all the five religious communities, Jains are using pressure cooker for cooking pulses which preserves nutrients and most of the Muslims are using boiling method which leads to loss of nutrients. Only a small percentage (31-55%) of the other Religious communities are using pressure cooker.

With regard to the cooking vegetables, in all the religious communities, majority of the families (78-100%) are practising boiling and frying and frying methods. Boiling method is used mostly by Christians (40%), Hindus (36%) and Jains (20%) while Sikhs and Muslims use it the least (5-6%). Steaming method of cooking vegetables is more practised among the Jains, Sikhs and Christians (50-60%) compared to the Muslim and Hindu families (15-29%).

A higher percentage (55-60%) of the respondents with the exception of Muslims washed vegetables before cutting them. Only among the Muslims, 73 per cent of the families washed vegetables after cutting them. It can be stated on the whole that 60 per cent of the Jains and about 50 per cent of the Sikhs, Christians and Hindus follow the method of washing vegetables and then cutting them. Similar trend can be noticed with the amount of water used for cooking vegetables. More than 60 per cent of Jains, Sikhs, Christians and Hindus use sufficient water to cook vegetables. It is only among the Muslim families that 64 per cent of them use excess water to cook vegetables.

To conclude, from the observations on food preparation and cooking methods practised among the various religious groups, a higher percentage of the Muslim families follow traditional and undesirable methods. This may be the consequence of their relatively lower economic status and higher illiteracy rate. To a large extent, highly polished rice is consumed by all the communities., The use of pressure cookers for cooking rice, pulses and vegetables is followed more by Jains and Christians. The consumption of parboiled rice, however is very limited among all the families. Majority of the them did not consume rice conjee. Some of them wash vegetables after cutting them which can lead a loss of vitamins. However, many families neither adopted pressure cooking which prevents the loss of nutrients nor did they possess nutritional knowledge necessary to conserve the nutrients. The traditional methods of cooking among families which practice them need to be changed by appropriate nutrition education programmes.

Religious Restrictions on Food Among Different Religious Communities

In each society a considerable amount of time, energy and wealth are allocated to religious activities. There are ceremonial and ritual feasts. Objects are used in the actual rituals. There is ritual preparation as well as destruction of objects, property, food etc. Many investigators are spending a considerable amount of time in actually observing such religious patterns *(Goode, 1951).*

All over the world, various religions have profound influence on man's dietary practices and customs. Over the centuries, many religions have decreased what foods could not eat on certain days of the year. Many of these dietary habits have become symbols of the religions themselves.

Information on percentage of families following religious restrictions on food among different religious communities is presented in Table—4.22.

The results of the present survey show that the majority of families are following religious restrictions. Jains, Christians and Muslims are observing religious restrictions to a greater extent than Sikhs and Hindus.

Table—4.22 Percentage of Families Following Religious Restrictions on Food

Religion	Following the Religious Restrictions	
	Yes	No
Jain	100.00 (10)	—
Sikh	75.00 (15)	25.00 (5)
Christian	90.00 (18)	10.00 (2)
Muslim	98.00 (98)	2.00 (2)
Hindu	65.00 (325)	35.00 (175)

A list of the foods restricted among the different communities is presented below. The reasons for doing so are also presented.

Religion	Foods	Reasons
1. Jain	Roots and Tubers	Because they grow underground
	Non-vegetarian foods	Ahimsa
2. Sikh	Chicken Pork Beef	Advocated in their sacred book "Granth"
3. Christian	Blood	Bible advocates the restriction
	Beetroot	It looks like blood.
4. Muslim	Pork	Advocated in their sacred book "Khuran".
	Snake gourd Pumpkin	Unknown

(Contd...)

5. Hindu		
Non-vegetarian	Beef	Consider cow as a sacred animal
Vegetarians (Brahmins and Vysyas)	Onions Garlics	Strong and smelly foods to be avoided as per religious dictates
Non-vegetarian foods		Ahimsa.

Among the Jains, all the families are strictly vegetarian as per their religious restrictions. A large per cent of the Sikh families also follow religious restrictions. They do not eat foods that are specified to be avoided in their sacred book 'Granth'. Majority of the Christian families are also following religious restrictions inspite of their higher educational status. However, the foods which they do not consume are few normally blood and beetroot. Compared to all the other religions, it may be concluded that Christian religion has the least restrictions and this may lead to better practices of the people from the nutrition point of view.

Many of the Muslim families strictly observe their religious restrictions as is the case among some Hindu families. It is among the Muslims and Hindus that the religious restrictions significantly affect the dietary practices of the people specially among the low income groups who are also illiterate. On the whole it may be concluded that a large per cent of the families still observe religious restrictions with regard to food.

Food Beliefs and Superstitions Among Different Religious Communities

A study of food beliefs and superstitions is essential as these findings would be useful for educational programmes aiming to improve the nutritional status of various groups.

Solien and Scrimshaw (1957) indicated that it is important to collect information about food beliefs and superstitions for nutrition education programmes intended to change food habits.

As in nearly every part of the world, among all the five religious communities covered in the present survey there are beliefs that some foods are hot, some are cold and some may be flatulence causing. In Table—4.23 the related information is presented. The highest per cent of families having beliefs and superstitions is Muslims, while the lowest per cent is among Christians. The higher educational status of the Christians than among Muslims may explain this situation. A list of the foods generally avoided by the Jain, Sikh, Christian, Muslim and Hindu communities is given.

Table—4.23 Food Beliefs and Superstitions Existing Among Different Religious Communities

Religion	Per cent of families having the beliefs and superstitions		Beliefs and superstition on combination of foods	
	Yes	No	Yes	No
Jain	60.00 (6)	40.00 (4)	—	100.00 (10)
Sikh	45.00 (9)	55.00 (11)	40.00 (8)	60.00 (12)
Christian	35.00 (7)	65.00 (13)	55.00 (11)	45.00 (9)
Muslim	67.00 (67)	33.00 (33)	71.00 (71)	29.00 (29)
Hindu	65.20 (326)	34.80 (174)	64.20 (321)	35.80 (179)

The foods avoided by the five religious communities are common among the three categories—Heat producing, cold producing and flatulence causing. However, the Jains avoid additionally onions, cabbage and ladies finger as flatulence causing.

The list of combinations of foods avoided shows that Jains do not have any superstitions on combinations of foods as they are vegetarians while the combinations have one non-vegetarian food or the other.

List of Foods Avoided as per Beliefs and Superstitions Among Different Religious Communities

S. No.	Heat Producing Foods	Cold Producing Foods	Flatulence Causing Foods
1.	Drumstick	Bottle gourd	Potatoes
2.	Ladies finger	Snake gourd	Colacasia
3.	Brinjal	Ridge gourd	Eggs
4.	Papaya	Cucumber	Green chillies
5.	Horsegram	Radish	Sweet potato
6.	Goat meat	Sweet limes	Bengalgram
7.	Jaggery	Greengram	Carrot
8.	Cluster beans	Tomatoes	Beetroot
9.	Eggs	Water melon	Jowar
10.	Bengalgram		**Jains:**
11.	Bajra		Onions
12.	Wheat		Cabbage
13.	Mangoes		Ladies finger
14.	Gogu leaves		
15.	Jack Fruit		
16.	Raw plantain		
17.	Sesame (or) gingelly		

Hot foods are avoided during fevers and cold foods are avoided during colds and coughs. It may be observed from the list that Cucumber, Radish and Ridge gourd which are cheap and seasonally available are believed to be cold foods and are avoided especially during colds. Even families belonging to low income groups are holding these beliefs and superstitions. On the one hand they cannot afford to purchase expensive vegetables freely due to shortage of money and on the other they are not eating foods within their reach due to certain beliefs and superstitions. Thus their diets are mainly deficient of vegetables, which are the chief sources of vitamins and minerals. In the same way potatoes, eggs, carrots, beetroots etc., are avoided as they are believed to produce flatulence. Thus inspite of availability sometimes misconceptions about food deter them from using these foods. This is mainly due to lack of education, nutritional knowledge and culture. As *Byrne et al, (1962)* indicated major cultural factors obstructing nutritional food intake are beliefs, fears, taboos and superstitions about food.

Superstitions Regarding the Combination of Foods Among Four Different Religious Communities

S.No.	Combination of Foods	Reasons
1.	Snake gourd + Egg	When these particular dishes are combined and consumed, they become poisonous and thus are harmful to the body
2.	Fish + Egg	
3.	Meat + Fish	
4.	Meat + Potatoes	
5.	Fish + Curds	

Nutritional Practices During Special Conditions (Pregnancy and Lactation) Among Different Religious Communities

The kind of food people eat is the result, not only of ecology, agriculture, income, occupation etc., but also of culture. The various cultural factors influencing food intake during special conditions is to be considered in a study of nutritional patterns.

The following is a discussion of various socio-cultural attitude and habits of women relating to foods during pregnancy and lactation. The socio-cultural aspects concerning food as presented here with reference to pregnant and lactating women reflect the various ideas and beliefs that the women hold about the functions of a variety of food items and their effects.

Food Patterns During Pregnancy

It is important to look at the nutritional status of the female prior to pregnancy as well as during pregnancy. During pregnancy a woman should eat a wide variety of body building food and strictly follow health rules. The pregnant women should not neglect their physical needs as two lives are involved. In this context, the women respondents of the present study were interviewed for food practices during pregnancy and lactation. The women of all the five religious communities were interviewed. The information secured is presented in Table—4.24.

Of the 650 women surveyed 40 per cent believed that certain foods should be specially consumed during pregnancy. They stated that consumption of certain foods is very good for the health of the mother and the growth of the baby.

From Table—4.24 it may be seen that a higher per cent (90%) of the Jain families followed by Hindu (41%), Christian (40%), Muslim (31%) and Sikh (20%) families had beliefs about recommending certain foods for pregnant women. The lists of foods recommended and beliefs expressed are presented for Jains separately since they do not consume flesh foods and have recommended some different foods from those of the other religious groups.

Table—4.24 Percentage of Women Recommending and Restricting Specific Foods During Pregnancy and Lactation, Among Different Religious Communities

Physiological status	Jain	Sikh	Christian	Muslim	Hindu	Total
Pregnancy						
Foods recom-mended	90.00 (9)	20.00 (4)	40.00 (8)	31.00 (31)	41.40 (207)	39.85 (259)
Foods restricted	50.00 (5)	35.00 (7)	30.00 (6)	75.00 (75)	54.60 (273)	56.31 (366)
Lactation						
Foods recom-mended	100.00 (10)	35.00 (7)	50.00 (10)	65.00 (65)	69.80 (349)	67.85 (441)
Foods restricted	100.00 (10)	45.00 (9)	40.00 (8)	77.00 (77)	70.60 (353)	70.31 (457)

Among the foods recommended almost all foods such as meat, milk, fruits and garlic are very good for the mother and the baby. Other foods mentioned are harmless and may not have any negative effect. But, most of the foods recommended are expensive. Since a large per cent of the population surveyed belong to middle income (65%) and low income (13%) groups, they may not consume the foods in adequate amounts and frequencies. Foods such as mangoes and apples are totally out of reach of low income groups and so is the case with special foods desired to satisfy the carvings of pregnant women. However, foods such as banana and rice are the food items which are within the reach of majority of pregnant women and have the overall positive effect of contributing calories if not necessarily a variety of nutrients.

Though the foods recommended are nutritious the functions stated are nonspecific and not scientific. Protein rich foods like meat and milk for example have been stated to provide energy. This indicates a lack of nutrition knowledge among the respondents. False beliefs are expressed such as coconut for large eyes and milk with kumkuma poovu for good complexion. These beliefs need to be eliminated by relevant education.

Foods Recommended During Pregnancy by Jain Women

Foods	Functions and Beliefs Expressed
1. Milk	It gives energy to the body
2. Fruits like orange, apple, banana	They prevent dizziness and fainting and also good for health
3. Kunkuma poovu with milk	Child will have good complexion
4. Coconut	Child will have large eyes
5. Badami milk	Child will have good complexion

Foods Recommended During Pregnancy by Sikh, Christian, Muslim and Hindu Women

Foods	Functions and Beliefs Expressed
1. Milk	It gives energy to the body.
2. Fruits like orange, apple, banana	They prevent dizziness and fainting and also good for health
3. Meat, fish	Needed for energy
4. Garlic	Good for digestion
5. Soda water	Cures many illnesses
6. Kumkuma poovu with milk	Child will have good complexion

With reference to foods restricted during pregnancy, fifty six per cent of the total number of women surveyed believe that some food items should be restricted to pregnant women. Fifty per cent of Jain, 35 per cent of Sikh, 30 per cent of Christian, 75 per cent of Muslim and 54.6 per cent of the Hindu women (Table—4.24) stated specifically that certain food items should be restricted if the pregnant women and the offspring have to be hale and healthy.

It can be noted that among all the religious communities, a large per cent (76%) of the Muslim families are imposing restrictions on the consumption of various food items during pregnancy. Contrary to this group, only 30 per cent of the Christians are doing so.

Foods Restricted During Pregnancy Among Women of Five Religious Groups

Foods	Beliefs Expressed
1. Eggs	Should not be eaten during the latter half of pregnancy. Causes abortion. Child will be born with bald head.
2. Papaya	Causes abortion
3. Root vegetables specially potato, bengalgram	Causes flatulence and discomfort.
4. Black foods like grapes, jambu fruits, nuts	'Nalla Chevva' diseases will come (or) child will be born with a dark complexion.
5. Egg Plant	Skin allergy
6. Leafy vegetables	Baby becomes skinned
7. Spicy foods	Make a pregnant woman's blood come out.
8. Pumpkin	Labour pains will increase
9. Custard apple, pine apple and horsegram.	These are too hot and lead to abortion

Most of the foods restricted are inexpensive and nutritious. It is ironic that while foods that are nutritious, inexpensive and within reach of the population are restricted foods which are expensive and out of reach of the majority of population are recommended.

The beliefs stated for each food have no scientific explanation. However they, prevent a woman from consuming the foods that are available to her. Common and inexpensive vegetables like pumpkin, and leafy vegetables are restricted while eggs, horsegram and bengalgram are not acceptable in this state of life. The belief about custard apple is interesting because it is avoided as it is hot and may result in abortion. Beliefs and restrictions of this type adversely affect a pregnant woman. Lack of proper nourishment of the mother may in turn affect the growth of the baby. Therefore, it is essential that proper measures be taken to see that these beliefs and practices are not followed in future.

Food Patterns During Lactation

Foods recommended during lactation by various religious communities are listed along with the beliefs, the women hold regarding different foods. Lactating women are expected to follow dietary patterns which delete a number of food items from the menu and they are expected to eat as little food as possible. She is considered to be unwell and is treated and fed as sparingly as a sick person. Since many people believe that there is a connection between mother's diet and infant's health during lactation, they promote limited eating so that the infant is less likely to come to harm. However, certain foods are recommended to be added to the diet of a lactating women. The beliefs hold are mostly related to maintenance of health and promotion of lactation.

Sixty eight per cent of the families surveyed believed that certain foods should be given to the lactating mothers so that the specific food items will enable the mother not only to produce more milk but also promote health of the mother and child.

Recommended Foods During Lactation Among Five Religious Communities

Foods	Functions/Beliefs
1. Betel leaves	*(a)* They promote lactation and are generally good for the mother
	(b) Help digestion and heal wounds
	(c) Stop thirst
2. Dry ginger, pepper and jaggery, 'raw sugar'	Good for stomach pain
3. Milk and curds	They cool the body.
4. Dried fish, garlic, meat	Enable the mother to produce more milk.
5. Rice water from the previous day mixed with salt or ragi to be given after delivery	Prevents fever, shivering, fits or pus formation internally.
6. Garlic	Prevents the mother from getting fits.

Some of the beliefs regarding foods for lactating mothers have positive connotations eventhough their nutritional value may be limited. All the Jains, 35 per cent of Sikhs, 50 per cent of Christians, 65 per cent of Muslims and 70 per cent of Hindus recommended the consumption of specific foods during lactation. A higher per cent of the Jains recommended consumption of certain specific foods not only during pregnancy but also during lactation. Some of the foods like betel leaves will not increase the nutritional intake of the lactating mother. However, since betel leaves are plentiful, cheap and easily acquired, they are used. Some beliefs promote the use of nutritious foods such as chicken, dried fish, meat, milk and milk products and garlic.

Regarding foods restricted during lactation, of the 650 families belonging to various religious communities, 70 per cent believe that some food items should be restricted during lactation period. Among the total families studied 100 per cent of Jains, 45 per cent of Sikhs, 40 per cent of Christians, 77 per cent of Muslims and 79 per cent of Hindus believe in imposing restrictions on the diet taken by the lactating mothers. It can be observed that Jains, Muslims and Hindus follow restrictions on food to a greater extent than Sikhs and Christians.

Below are some of the classified beliefs that can affect the nutrient intake of a lactating woman. The restrictions on her diet are numerous. The most commonly accepted reasoning for these dictatry restrictions is that while a woman is resting in bed after delivery and is not expending much energy, her systems would not be able to digest many foods consumed, that she may catch a cold or get fevers if she eats well after delivery.

Foods Restricted During Lactation Among Jain Community

Foods	Beliefs
1. Potato, bottle gourd, mango, jack fruit and guavas	It may cause the child to have fits which may even turn out to be fatal.
2. Brinjal, Ladies fingers	They are heat producing foods
3. Roots, vegetables	Flatulence causing foods

The foods which are recommended are expensive and would be difficult for people belonging to lower economic status to consume frequently. Same trend may be observed in the case of foods restricted and recommended during pregnancy. This trend suggests that nutrition education be given to the population in general so that good nutritional practices are followed during pregnancy and lactation.

Restricted Food Practices During Lactation Among Sikh, Christian, Muslim and Hindu Communities

	Food Practices	Beliefs
1.	Night meal avoided	If night meal is taken it will lead to indigestion
2.	Mutton avoided	If eaten after delivery it will create trouble
3.	Egg avoided	It is a cold food so, it may lead to delirium
4.	During the first thirty days after delivery milk and curds to be avoided	They may cause fits either in the mother, in the child or may lead to indigestion
5.	Left over foods are avoided	They harm the health of the child.
6.	Solid foods to be avoided during the first few days after delivery.	If eaten may result in fever, indigestion or some other physical irregularity.
7.	More than one rice meal a day for the first forty days after delivery.	Will cause stomach trouble.
8.	Vegetables avoided.	If eaten, the wounds of the uterus take a long time to heal and may even turn septic.
9.	Pulses and legumes not to be eaten upto one month after delivery.	Child's digestive system gets affected resulting in diarrhoea.

(Contd...)

10. Egg and mutton avoided.	Consumption of these will adversely affect the baby.
11. Egg and jack fruit to be avoided	Consumption of these may result in fits in the child.
12. Cold foods such as egg, banana, sweet lime and curds, to be avoided after delivery	If taken, the baby will catch a cold.
13. Brinjal, pumpkin, bottle gourd, green plantain, peas, potato, mango and guava avoided	If taken, can harm the child in many ways like gas formation, fits, itching/ scratching.

It is unfortunate that numerous foods are restricted which are actually nutritious and good for both the mother and the child. Many vegetables which are commonly available at cheap prices are restricted. All these beliefs adversely affect the vulnerable group of lactating mothers.

From the above it is clear that a lactating woman is not able to have her usual meals even after the initial period of lactation is over. For time periods varying anywhere from three to forty days she is allowed only one meal a day instead of two. Even after the commencement of one meal she has to avoid many foods such as rice, meat, eggs, fish, milk products either individually or in varying combinations for differing lengths of time.

From the Table—4.24, it may be observed that a higher percentage of the Jain families are adhering to dietary recommendations during pregnancy and lactation as well as to restrictions on various food items. In constrast to the other religious groups, it is among the Christian families, that a smaller per cent are following restrictions imposed on food during pregnancy and lactation. This may be attributed to a higher educational and occupational status prevalent in this community. Restriction on various food items during pregnancy and lactation are followed by a large per cent of Muslims and Hindus and to a relatively lesser extent by Sikh families. The reason for a large per cent of Muslims and Hindus following these undesirable practices may be attributed to their low educational status, poor economic background and a strict and blind adherence to traditional cultural practices.

It may be concluded that the people in the religious communities surveyed generally connect food with health. However, the rationale behind the use of foods is unscientific and can lead to practices harmful to health. There is a dearth in nutrition knowledge in that the perception of the functions of foods is erroneous. The causes of diseases are traced back to certain types of foods and the view that avoidance of those foods will prevent the illness is upheld. The consequence of this reasoning is restrictions on most of the nutritions foods, which can promote the health of both the mother and child. There is a great need for nutrition and health education to promote better practices with scientific reasoning.

Child Rearing Practices Among Different Religious Communities

Child rearing practices differ from one social group to another. Some mothers may have access to scientific information that would influence their child rearing practices, while some others may carry on age old traditions. In *Garner's (1965),* opinion, patterns of child rearing differ from one group to another. In India there are a number of social groups. The present survey examines the child rearing practices of five religious groups. The child rearing practices studied include infant feeding practices and utilisation of mid day meal scheme.

Of the infant feeding practices, keeping in view the importance of breast feeding, its prevalence among the five religious communities—Jain, Sikh, Christian, Muslim and Hindu—was first examined. It is a well known fact that there is no better food for the baby than mother's milk. It contains all the nutrients the baby needs. Mother's milk is clean, cheap and easily obtainable. It is, infact, the food nature planned for the baby to have. It contains in correct proportions most of the nutrients necessary for the baby. During the first two or three days after the birth of the baby the breast does not secrete milk but yields a yellowish fluid called colostrum. Colostrum is good for the baby and takes care of its first hunger. But, in some parts of India there is a belief that colostrum is harmful and therefore the baby is fed sugar water. Actually colostrum is richer in body building nutrients than mature milk itself and provides valuable nutrients lacking in milk and needed for the protection of the baby against infectious diseases.

The findings presented in Table—4.25 show that all the mothers of Jain community breast feed their babies. Fifty per cent of them started feeding the baby on the second day, while 20 per cent of them fed the baby on the first day and another 30 per cent of them on the third day. Majority of the Jains stated that breast feeding was good for the baby. They opined that the ideal duration of breast feeding was 12 months and some said that it was 18 months. However, 30 per cent of the mothers stopped breast feeding after 7-12 months, while half of them breast fed their baby upto 13-24 months. Only a small per cent (20%) stopped breast feeding before 6 months. Keeping in view the growing needs of the baby, 40 per cent of the Jain mothers weaned their infants as early as 3 months and by 6 months all the mothers were giving supplemental foods to the baby along with breast milk.

Among the Sikhs one mother did not breast feed her child, while 35 per cent of the mothers breast fed on the first day and another 35 per cent on the third day. A quarter of them started breast feeding on the 2nd day. However a

Table—4.25 Infant Feeding Practices Among Different Religious Communities

Religion	Initiation of Breast Feeding					Duration of Breast Feeding (Months)				
	1st day	2nd day	3rd day	Later	Not fed	6	12	18	24	36 & above
Jain	20.00 (2)	50.00 (5)	30.00 (3)	–	–	–	80.00 (8)	20.00 (2)	–	–
Sikh	35.00 (7)	25.00 (5)	35.00 (7)	–	5.00 (1)	–	35.00 (7)	35.00 (7)	25.00 (5)	5.00 (1)
Christian	35.00 (7)	25.00 (5)	30.00 (6)	–	10.00 (2)	15.00 (3)	30.00 (6)	35.00 (7)	20.00 (4)	–
Muslim	13.00 (13)	18.00 (18)	64.00 (64)	4.00 (4)	1.00 (1)	5.00 (5)	43.00 (43)	10.00 (10)	32.00 (32)	10.00 (10)
Hindu	16.00 (80	24.40 (122)	54.00 (270)	3.40 (17)	2.20 (11)	5.80 (29)	40.60 (203)	22.00 (110)	22.40 (112)	9.20 (46)

(Contd...)

(Table—4.25 Contd...)

Religion	Discontinuance of Breast Feeding (Months)						Age at Weaning (Months)						
	6	7-12	13-24	25-36	37 and above	Not fed	3	5	6	9	12	15	18
Jain	20.00 (2)	30.00 (3)	50.00 (5)	–	–	–	40.00 (4)	10.00 (1)	50.00 (5)	–	–	–	–
Sikh	40.00 (8)	40.00 (8)	5.00 (1)	10.00 (2)	–	5.00 (1)	20.00 (4)	30.00 (6)	35.00 (7)	15.00 (3)	–	–	–
Christian	15.00 (3)	45.00 (9)	20.00 (4)	10.00 (2)	–	10.00 (2)	50.00 (10)	10.00 (2)	30.00 (6)	10.00 (2)	–	–	–
Muslim	7.00 (7)	21.00 (21)	43.00 (43)	20.00 (20)	8.00 (8)	1.00 (1)	8.00 (8)	25.00 (25)	33.00 (33)	19.00 (19)	15.00 (15)	–	–
Hindu	13.60 (68)	30.20 (151)	32.60 (163)	19.40 (97)	2.00 (10)	2.20 (11)	14.00 (70)	22.40 (112)	38.80 (194)	13.00 (65)	9.40 (47)	1.00 (5)	1.40 (7)

third of them stated that ideal breast feeding time was 12 months while another third of them said it was 18 months. There were some mothers who said it was about 24-36 months. But majority of them stopped breast feeding their child after 7-12 months. Only a small per cent breast fed upto 13-24 and more months. Majority of the mothers weaned their baby in the fifth or sixth month. Small per cent of them weaned their baby in the 3rd month, while some did so in the 9th month.

In the Christian community, two mothers did not breast feed their baby. In initiation of breast feeding and in ideal period of breast feeding, the trend was more or less the same as that observed among Sikhs. However, a little less than half of the Christian mothers breast fed their babies upto 7-12 months while a half of them weaned their baby in the third month itself. Only a small per cent did so in the ninth month. Compared to other religious groups, the majority of Christian mothers practised early weaning. This is in keeping with their higher educational status.

Among the Muslim and Hindu communities more or less same trend can be noticed. In both the Communities, more than half of the mothers started breast feeding on the third day thus foregoing the advantages of colostrum. Majority of them reported that the ideal period of breast feeding is one year. Most of them breast feed the baby upto 7-12 months and 13-24 months. These are the two Communities where some mothers breast feed even upto three years and above and greater per cent weaned their baby in the 9th month or beyond within the Community. However, the majority of the mothers weaned their baby either in the fifth or sixth month.

Comparing all the religious communities, it may be concluded that a higher per cent of the Sikh and Christian mothers started breast feeding their babies in the first day with 50 per cent of the Jain mothers doing so on the second day. All the Jains breast feed their babies, while a small per cent of the mothers in the other communities resorted to other feeding practices. Majority of women of the different communities breast feed either upto 7-12 months or 13-24 months. While a higher per cent of the Jains and Christians wean the baby in the 3rd month. The majority of the other communities did so either in the 5th or in the 6th month.

Only among some of the Muslim and Hindu communities weaning began as late as 12 to 18 months. On the whole breast feeding practice is widely prevalent among the different religious groups. The Jain, Sikh and Christian Communities appreciated the feeding of colostrum to the baby to a greater extent than the others. While 100 per cent of Jains, 85 per cent of Sikhs and 90 per cent of Christians weaned their children by the 6th month, only 66 per cent and 75 per cent of Muslim and Hindu communities respectively weaned their children by the 6th month. It can be said that better infant feeding practices are being followed among Jain, Sikh and Christian communities as compared to Muslim and Hindu communities.

With the exception of the Jain community, some of the mothers in the other four religious communities resorted to feeding practices other than breast feeding. Even among the Jains, the babies were fed with other types of milk after one year. Table—4.26 gives the information on other milk foods used and the method of feeding among different religious communities.

Among the Jains after one year babies were fed with other types of milk. Feeding bottle was used by all the mothers. A large per cent fed their babies with cow's milk. Also the majority sterilised the bottle before each feed. Similar trend may be noticed among the Sikhs. Here 40 per cent of them used commercial milk powders and all used feeding bottle. They started feeding the baby with other types of milk after one year and some after one and half to two years.

Table—4.26 Percentage Distribution of Different Religious Communities as per Type of Milk Used and Feeding Methods

Religion	Types of milk			Mode of feeding	
	Cow's	Buffalo's	Commercial	Uggu ginne	Feeding bottle
Jain	60.00 (6)	10.00 (1)	30.00 (3)	–	100.00 (10)
Sikh	40.00 (8)	20.00 (4)	40.00 (8)	–	100.00 (20)
Christian	15.00 (3)	20.00 (4)	65.00 (13)	–	100.00 (20)
Muslim	16.00 (16)	52.00 (52)	32.00 (32)	23.00 (23)	100.00 (100)
Hindu	12.80 (64)	43.80 (219)	43.40 (217)	9.00 (45)	100.00 (500)

(Contd...)

(Table—4.26 Contd...)

Religion	Age of using							Sterilising the Bottle	
	Uggu ginne (months)		Feeding Bottle (Months)					Yes	No.
	3	6	6	12	18	24	36		
Jain	–	–	–	20.00 (2)	50.00 (5)	30.00 (3)	–	80.00 (8)	20.00 (2)
Sikh	–	–	–	20.00 (4)	45.00 (9)	30.00 (6)	5.00 (1)	75.00 (15)	25.00 (5)
Christian	–	–	–	55.00 (11)	35.00 (7)	10.00 (2)	–	85.00 (17)	15.00 (3)
Muslim	23.00 (23)	–	2.00 (2)	43.00 (43)	31.00 (31)	15.00 (15)	9.00 (9)	54.00 (54)	46.00 (46)
Hindu	9.00 (45)	–	3.40 (17)	39.40 (197)	43.20 (216)	11.00 (55)	3.00 (15)	42.20 (211)	57.80 (289)

Seventy five per cent of them sterilised the feeding bottle before use.

In the Christian Community the highest per cent of the mothers fed commercial milk after one year using sterilised feeding bottles. Sterilisation was practised more in this Community than among the other communities.

It is among the Muslim and Hindu communities that a higher per cent of the mothers used buffalo's milk to feed their babies. While majority of them fed their baby after one year some did so before 6 months also. However, this was due to lack of breast milk among the mothers. This is in accordance with their lower economic status and possible consumption of less nutritious foods by the mothers. It is in these two communities that the traditional mode of feeding with uggu ginne is practised as early as the third month. The feeding bottle was also used by all the mothers. The practice of sterilisation of feeding bottle is much less prevalent in these two communities as compared to the others. About 50 per cent of the respondents reported not sterilising the bottle.

Comparing all the communities, it may be stated that Jains apart from breast feeding also resorted to other sources of milk. A large per cent of them used sterilised feeding bottles and cow's milk at 12 months and above. A high percentage of the Christians used commercial milk powders and also used sterilised feeding bottles. The lowest per cent of mothers using sterilised bottles was among the Muslim and Hindu. These two communities used buffalo's milk to a greater extent. The feeding of other milk foods was started earlier among the Muslim and Hindu communities as compared to the other three communities.

With a view to securing the opinion of mothers among the five religious communities about the mid-day meal scheme, which was introduced by the government in schools in the year of 1983. Questions were asked concerning the participation of their children in the mid-day meal scheme and reasons for non-participation if the children did not consume the food given under the scheme. The mothers were also questioned on whether they encourage their children to buy snacks at school.

The information obtained is presented in Table—4.27. The Jain families send their children to convent schools where mid-day meal scheme is not operative. Lunch is either sent to school or the children come home for lunch. Seven per cent of the families do not give money to their children to buy tit-bits at school. Religious restrictions and the higher economic status of the families prevent them from sending the children to schools where mid-day meals are provided. They do not encourage their children to buy snacks at school on health grounds.

Considering the other four communities, it may be observed that the children are sent to different schools, where they mix with cosmopolitan groups and where mid-day meal scheme is operative in some schools. A greater number of Muslim and Hindu communities send their children to cosmopolitan schools.

In the Sikh community, 40 per cent sent their children to schools where mid-day meals are given. However, only 20 per cent allowed their children to partake of these meals, while the others felt that it was below their status to do so and that the food may affect the health of their child. A higher per cent of the Sikhs also did not give money to their children to buy snacks.

Among the Christians, only 5 per cent allowed their children to eat food under the mid-day meal scheme, though 30 per cent sent their children to schools where mid-day meal scheme was in implementation. The remaining 25 per cent

Table—4.27 Extent of Participation of Children in Mid-day Meal Scheme and Reasons for Non-participation

Religion	Mid-day Meal Existing		Allow Participation	
	Yes	No	Yes	No
Jain	–	100.00 (10)	–	–
Sikh	40.00 (8)	60.00 (12)	20.00 (4)	20.00 (4)
Christian	30.00 (6)	70.00 (14)	5.00 (1)	25.00 (5)
Muslim	67.00 (67)	33.00 (33)	46.00 (46)	21.00 (21)
Hindu	56.40 (282)	43.60 (218)	35.80 (179)	20.60 (103)

(Contd...)

(Table—4.27 Contd...)

Religion	Reasons for Non-participation			Money for Snacks	
	Prestige	Child Health Aspect	Any Other	Yes	No
Jain	–	–	–	30.00 (3)	70.00 (7)
Sikh	5.00 (1)	15.00 (3)	–	40.00 (8)	60.00 (12)
Christian	–	25.00 (5)	–	25.00 (5)	75.00 (15)
Muslim	4.00 (4)	16.00 (16)	1.00 (1)	73.00 (73)	27.00 (27)
Hindu	3.40 (17)	15.60 (78)	1.60 (8)	66.40 (332)	33.60 (168)

felt that their child's health would be adversely affected by the food given under the scheme. It was observed by this investigator that the food provided under the scheme is of poor quality and not clean. These families also did not encourage their children to buy snacks since they were of the opinion that food brought outside the home is not clean and that it may affect the health of the children.

A larger percentage of the Muslims and Hindus allowed their children to eat food given in schools. Of those who did not permit their children to partake of the mid-day meal, only a small per cent felt that it was a prestige issue. Most of the families felt that the food would affect their children's health. A high per cent of the Muslim and Hindu women gave money to their children to eat snacks. It may be noted that the majority of the Muslim and Hindu families belong to the low income group and the per cent of illiterates is also high in these communities. The low socio-economic status may be partly responsible for the mothers permitting the children to eat at school and to purchase snacks from vendors.

Jains send their children exclusively to convent schools where mid-day meal scheme is not implemented, while a high per cent of the Muslim and Hindu families send their children to various schools where mid-day meal is operative in more than 50 per cent of the schools.

The Christian and Sikh children attend schools, a few of which have the mid-day meal programme. Jains do not encourage their children to eat away from home either at school or at the snack vendering stalls. The Christians stand next in discouraging their children eating away from home followed by the Sikhs. The Muslims and Hindus on the other hand are not as restrictive in allowing their children to buy snacks at the vendors or to participate in mid-day meal scheme. The majority of families of all religious communities, who restrict their children eating away from home are doing so because they are of the opinion that food from external sources is harmful to the children's health.

Prevalence of Undesirable Habits Among Different Religious Communities

In the present study chewing betel and tobacco, smoking and drinking alcohol have been listed as undesirable habits.

Undesirable habits affect the dietary habits and these in turn affect health. Poor health can affect nutritional status. Smoking, tobacco chewing and drinking alcohol are some of the habits which are definitely harmful to health. The extent of prevalence of these habits among the five religious communities was surveyed in the present investigation. The data on percentage prevalence of undesirable habits among different religious communities is presented in Table—2.8. The respondents view on the relationship of these habits to health and eating practices was also obtained.

Out of the 650 families surveyed, 24 per cent are found to chew betel leaves, tobacco, to smoke and drink alcohol. The habits of smoking and drinking alcohol pertain to men in the families while chewing betel and tobacco relate to both men and women. Many of the families stated that they can even forego their meals nut not these habits. It is stated that these habits stall hungers.

Among the Jains, inspite of their higher economic status, all of them are in the habit of chewing betel leaves. A thirty per cent of the men smoke eventhough they know that these habits can affect their health and eating patterns adversely. This information was obtained by some of the families from their doctor, while others were self informed. None of the Jains are in the habit of drinking alcohol or chewing tobacco.

Twenty five per cent of the Sikh men and women chewed betel leaves, 40 per cent of them had tobacco chewing and smoking habits and some of them (10%) even drank alcohol.

Table—4.28 Percentage Prevalence of Undesirable Habits Among Different Religious Communities

Religion	Other habits				Affect the health	
	Betel leaves	Tobacco	Smoking	Alcohol	Yes	No
Jain	100.00 (10)	–	30.00 (3)	–	70.00 (7)	30.00 (3)
Sikh	25.00 (5)	5.00 (1)	35.00 (7)	10.00 (2)	65.00 (13)	35.00 (7)
Christian	5.00 (1)	–	95.00 (19)	–	75.00 (15)	25.00 (5)
Muslim	31.00 (31)	80.00 (8)	51.00 (51)	10.00 (10)	42.00 (42)	58.00 (58)
Hindu	22.00 (110)	6.80 (34)	62.00 (310)	9.20 (46)	67.80 (339)	32.20 (161)

(Contd...)

(Table—4.28 Contd...)

Religion	Knowledge About the Health Hazards				Affect the Eating Practices	
	Friends	Doctor	Relatives	Self information	Yes	No
Jain	–	30.00 (3)	–	40.00 (4)	70.00 (7)	30.00 (3)
Sikh	25.00 (5)	15.00 (3)	5.00 (1)	15.00 (3)	35.00 (7)	65.00 (13)
Christian	–	30.00 (6)	15.00 (3)	15.00 (3)	40.00 (8)	60.00 (12)
Muslim	7.00 (7)	7.00 (7)	13.00 (13)	15.00 (15)	25.00 (25)	75.00 (75)
Hindu	15.60 (78)	21.80 (109)	8.80 (44)	21.60 (108)	51.60 (258)	48.40 (242)

Here also 65 and 35 per cent of the families knew about the adverse affect of these habits on health and dietary habits respectively. They obtained this information mostly from friends, doctors and relatives, while some of them (15 per cent) were self informed.

A negligible per cent (5%) of the Christian chewed betel leaves, while a very high per cent (95%) of them (men) smoked. But, none of them drank alcohol. Many of them (75%) knew about the adverse effects of these habits probably due to their high educational status.

Among Muslims and Hindus, the prevalence of undesirable habits is more or less similar. About 20 to 30 per cent chewed betel leaves, while 7 to 8 per cent of them chewed tobacco. Above 50 per cent had smoking habits and about 10 per cent drank alcohol in both communities. They did so inspite of knowing that these habits can affect their health and eating pattern. The causes for the formation of these habits can be many though the respondents often state that these habits help them to withstand hunger. These habits may also be attributed to their low economic and educational status. Many of the Muslim families did not know of the adverse effect of these habits on health and eating patterns. The Hindu families were better informed about the health hazards than the Muslim families. They secured this information from friends, doctors, relatives and on their own.

When the awareness to health hazards among the different communities is compared, it is observed that Jains and Christians are the best informed while Sikhs and Hindus are next best informed. The Muslims are at the lowest level in that only 42 per cent of them are aware of the health hazards of smoking and drinking alcohol and only 25 per cent are aware that these habits can affect eating practices. It is only among Jains and Christians that there is no prevalence of drinking alcohol and chewing tobacco.

5. Summary and Conclusions

Life styles of people differ with differing socio-economic, socio-cultural and religious background. Nutritional patterns occur in the context of the socio-economic and socio-cultural background of communities. The present investigation was undertaken to study the nutritional patterns of families belonging to five major religious communities of Tirupati.

A representative sample of six hundred and fifty families belonging to different religions; from twenty different wards of Tirupati town were selected by random sampling. The distribution as per religion was as follows: Jains-10, Sikhs-20, Christians-20, Muslims-100 and Hindus-500 families. A schedule partly structured and partly open-ended was piloted, finalised and administered to the housewives in an interview.

The major findings of the investigation are as follows:

The living conditions indicate that the majority of Jain, Sikh and Christian families live in comfort as compared to the Muslim and Hindu families. The Jains live in cement constructed houses with more than five rooms, while the other families live in two or three room houses. A large number of

Muslim families live in thatched, shed and tiled type of houses. The surroundings of majority of Muslim and Hindu households are unhygienic compared to those of the other religious groups. Lighting and ventilation are average for all the homes. Joint and extended family system prevails among the Jains to a greater extent than among the other groups. Nuclear families are predominant among Christians. Muslims have the largest family size compared to that of the other religious groups.

With regard to general health, the major illnesses reported for children are diarrhoea, common colds, cough and fever. The greater incidence of illness among children has been reported among Jains followed by Muslims, Hindus, Sikhs and Christians in that order. Among adults common colds, coughs and fever are more prevalent. The adults complained of diseases such as Diabetes, Gastric Ulcers and Cardiovascular diseases.

Regarding incidence of mortality among children, the lowest is recorded among Christian families and the highest among the Sikhs followed by Muslims, Jains and Hindus. The most common causes of Childhood deaths reported is diarrhoea. The Sikhs could not pinpoint the causes of death among their children.

Considering the educational status of women, Christians are the most highly educated. Also 100 per cent of them are educated. The Jain women are exclusive in that there is neither illiteracy nor collegiate education prevalent among them. They have mostly school education. Illiteracy is prevalent to a greater extent among the Muslims followed by Hindus and Sikhs. Collegiate and professional education is more among Sikhs and Hindus than among Muslims.

Comparing the educational status of men and women, men are more highly educated than women across all religious communities. This difference is more marked among Muslims than among the other communities. When illiteracy is considered while 50 per cent of Muslim women are illiterate only 22 per cent of the men are illiterate. Among Hindus, women are 24 per cent illiterates, while men are only 8 per cent illiterate. Among Sikhs only women are illiterate (15 per cent), while men are not. Even among Christians where all the women are educated the men have secured higher Post-graduate and professional degrees while women have reached upto graduate level only.

With regard to occupational status, the assumption that occupation is a consequence of education is confirmed in the Christian community. Forty per cent of Christian men are in the academic field. The Sikhs are mostly engaged in business. All the Jain families are in their traditional occupation of business even though 90 per cent of the men are educated upto plus two and graduate levels. It is among the Muslim community that the majority of the men are occupied with miscellaneous petty business. In the Hindu community, the men are in a variety of occupations.

The occupational status of the women is closely related to their educational status and culture. Among the Jains none of the women are in occupations other than household work. In contrast, most of the Christian women are engaged in fairly highly paid occupations such as teaching and nursing. Among the Sikhs only two of the women are employed and both are in high status occupations. Majority of Sikh, Muslim and Hindu women are exclusively in household work. The remaining are engaged, in diverse occupations like labour and petty business fetching low income.

The economic status of the families shows that irrespective of religion, majority of them belong to Rs. 5001-15,000 and 15,001-25,000 income levels. It is only among the Hindus and Jains that a few families belong to Rs. 45,000 and above income group. Christians are exclusive in that none belong to either the low income level of Rs. 5000 or high income levels of Rs. 35,001—45,000 and 45,001 and above. Among the Sikhs 5 per cent of them are in the Rs. 5001-

15,000 income group with another thirty per cent in Rs. 15,001-25,000. The majority of Muslims are at the low income levels of Rs. 5001-15,000. Of the five hundred Hindu families surveyed, 300 are in Rs. 5,001-15,000 and 15,001-25,000 income groups. This is the only community where families represent all grades of income.

The food expenditure patterns as per the income levels of the families show that an inverse relationship exists between income and expenditure. Among the Jains the per cent expenditure on food declines from 52 to 32 with increasing income. Similar pattern can be seen in the other communities, which is in accordance with Engle's law. The per cent expenditure on food among families belonging to the Muslim community is more at all the income levels especially in the Rs. 5,001-15,000 and 15,001-25,000 income levels when compared with that of other communities.

The per cent expenditure on different food groups shows that Jains in accordance with their religious practice of Lacto-vegetarianism are spending more on milk and milk products (Group V), vegetables and fruits (Group III) and fats and oils (Group IV) compared to the other communities. Among Sikhs and Hindus the expenditure pattern on different food groups is similar at different income levels. This similarity may probably be due to the close association of these communities over several decades. Most of the Muslims and Christians are non-vegetarians and consequently the expenditure on meat, fish and eggs (Group II) is the highest in these religious groups. Among all the communities the major expenditure is on staple foods (Group I), irrespective of income levels. However as income increases there is a decline in total expenditure on cereals (Group I) and an increase in expenditure on other food groups such as pulses, oils, fish, eggs, fruits etc. This is true of all the religious communities.

The food choices per day among families of different religious communities have been classified into three categories—regular, irregular and occasional, regular indicating a better choice and irregular and occasional indicating a poor choice. A greater percentage of the Jain, Sikh and Christian families are choosing foods in a more balanced manner as compared to the others. Among the Muslim and Hindu communities, 30 to 35 per cent of the families fall in the irregular/occasional groups. Therefore their choice of foods tends to be on a lower scale than that of the others, where only 10 to 25 per cent fall in the irregular/ occasional groups.

The menu plan of the five religious communities shows that the food preparations of Sikh, Christian, Muslim and Hindu communities are different from those of the Jain community. The food preparations of these four groups are mostly with rice, vegetables, root vegetables, non-vegetarian foods and to a relatively lesser extent with pulses and wheat. The various menu items of the Jains on the other hand are characterised by wheat, pulse and milk preparations using liberal amounts of fats and oils.

Festival expenditure on foods occupies an important place in the budget of every family irrespective of religion. This in itself indicates the significant influence of religious festivals on food habits. Cereals and pulses predominate in the special dishes prepared on festival days and these are in addition to the regular items consumed. In this way the special dishes may contribute to a certain extent to improve the nutritional status of the families.

With regard to preservation of foods, it can be seen that majority of the families are preserving foods. Most of the Jains follow pickling and sugar concentration methods of preserving foods, while more number of Christian families follow dehydration method. Muslims and Hindus preserve foods both by pickling and dehydration.

Considering cooking methods, more number of Jains and Christians use modern methods of cooking such as pressure cooking and non-straining of rice, pulses and vegetables. Majority of the Muslim families follow traditional and undesirable methods of cooking patterns. Among the Hindus 27 per cent of the families adopted pressure cooking and 14 per cent non-straining method. Sikhs closely follow the Hindus in these practices. Assessment of type of rice used showed that highly polished rice is used by all the communities and use of parboiled rice is very limited. Only a few Hindus and Muslims use parboiled rice as well as home pounded rice. None of the Jain, Sikh and Christian families do so.

Restrictions on certain foods as related to religious beliefs are prevalent among the majority of all the five religious groups. The Jains are strictly vegetarians and they avoid roots, tubers and non-vegetarian foods. Sikhs avoid chicken, pork and beef as advocated in the sacred "Granth", Christians avoid blood and beetroot. Muslims avoid pork, while Hindus avoid beef. The Brahmins among Hindus avoid onions and garlic.

Considering beliefs and superstitions related to foods irrespective of income levels, The highest per cent of families having these beliefs are Muslims (65%) while the lowest per cent is among Christians (35%). This may be related to the higher educational status of the Christians compared to that of the Muslims. Foods are labelled as heat producing, cold producing and flatulence causing and avoided during specific conditions like fevers, common colds. Among the low income groups, the cheaper and more nutritious foods are avoided due to beliefs and superstitions.

A survey of foods recommended and restricted during pregnancy and lactation shows that among all communities recommendations and restrictions exist. In the Christian community however a smaller per cent of families follow these practices. While the families connect these practices with the health of the mother and child, the rationale behind the promotion or restriction of foods is unscientific. There is restriction on many nutritious foods let alone restriction of the number of meals during lactation, which can be harmful to the health of the mother and the child. There is a dearth of nutrition and health information among the women of the different religious communities.

Infant and child rearing practices indicated that breast feeding is widely prevalent among the different religious groups. The Jain. Sikh and Christian communities feed colostrum to the baby to a greater extent than the other religious communities. A large per cent of the Jain, Sikh and Christian families also wean their children by the 6th month while only 66 and 75 per cent of Muslim and Hindu families respectively do so. Jains apart from breast feeding also use commercial milk powders or cow's milk and feed the babies with sterilised feeding bottles. The Muslim and Hindu families feed buffalo's milk additionally and use mostly unsterilised containers for feeding the children. It can be said that on the whole better feeding practices are being followed by Jains, Sikh and Christian communities as compared to that of Muslim and Hindu communities.

Regarding the rearing and feeding practices of children, the Jain families send their children to convent schools where mid-day meal scheme is not operative. These children either go home for lunch or get their meals sent to the schools. The children are also not allowed to by snacks at schools. Christians also discourage their children from eating away from home. The Sikhs are also fairly restrictive in their children participating in mid-day meal scheme. The Muslim and Hindu families however are not so strict and allow their children to participate in mid-day meal scheme as well as to buy snacks at the vendors. However, the majority of families which restrict the participation of their children in the mid-day meal scheme or from buying snacks at vendors, irrespective of religious affiliation do so as they believe that foods prepared away from home are unhygienic and can adversely affect the health of their children.

With regard to the prevalence of undesirable habits, of the total 650 families surveyed 25 per cent are found to chew betel leaves or tobacco, smoke and drink alcohol. All the Jains are in the habit of chewing betel leaves while a high per cent of the Christians (men) smoke. None of the members of the families in these two communities take alcohol. Sikhs on the other hand chew betel leaves, the men smoke and some even take alcohol. Among Muslim and Hindu communities a similar trend prevails. When the awareness to health hazards is compared, it is observed that Jains and Christians are more aware of health hazards of smoking and drinking alcohol, followed by Sikhs and Hindus. The Muslims are the least aware of health hazards of undesirable practices. Only 42 per cent of them have reported that tobacco chewing, smoking and alcohol affects health adversely.

Conclusions drawn from this investigation are as follows:

1. Nutritional patterns are closely associated with the socio-economic, socio-cultural status of the families among different religious communities of Tirupati.

2. Choice and frequency of choice of foods their preparation, cooking methods, menu plans and total expenditure on foods are all influenced by the income level of the families irrespective of religious affiliation. Better choice of foods, better cooking methods and more balanced meals occur as income increases. The total expenditure on foods bears an inverse relationship to income level. However, as income increases while the expenditure on staple cereals declines, the expenditure on quality foods such as fruits, vegetables, milk, milk products and fleshy foods increases. There is no bar on expenditure on foods during festivals. All families prepare special items at considered cost.

3. Religion and culture play a decisive role on the choice of foods and their preparations. The Jains are

vegetarians. They prepare more sweets and use wheat, milk and fats to a considerable degree in many preparations. Muslims and Christians are all non-vegetarians. They use flesh foods eggs, rice and pulses in many preparations. Muslims avoid pork. The Sikhs and Hindus are either non-vegetarian or vegetarian and they choose a variety of foods inclusive of rice, pulses and vegetables. There is a similarity in the types of preparations made among Sikhs and Hindus, who have lived in close association for several decades. Beef is avoided by both communities.

4. Educational status has a decisive influence on the occupational status and income level of the families. The well educated men and women of the families are better placed and earn more income, which in turn has an effect on the nutritional patterns.

5. Majority of Muslims occupy the lowest rung of the ladder with regard to education and income. Illiteracy prevails in this group. Many of them are engaged in petty business. The Christians on the other hand are the most highly educated and well placed as teachers, nurses, doctors and other. There is no illiteracy among them. The Jains are all literate though, not highly educated. They practice their traditional occupation of business fetching high income. They do not move into other types of occupation. The Sikhs and Hindus, a majority of them occupy a middle rung of the ladder with regard to education and income levels. They are more cosmopolitan in their outlook and in the occupations they choose. Illiteracy is prevalent in these groups but not to the extent seen among Muslims.

6. Considering the status of women across the different religious groups, it is observed that the Christian

women occupy the top position with regard to education and occupation. No women is illiterate. The Muslim women are at the lowest level in that a majority of them are illiterate and are engaged fully in household work. The Jain women though literate, have had only school education and they are all engaged as housewives. Therefore they are slightly better placed than Muslim women. The Hindu and Sikh women are above the Jain women in that many of them are better educated and have occupation other than household work alone.

7. Comparing the educational status of men and women, it is observed that women have a lower status than men among all religious communities.

8. Knowledge about nutrition, health and child rearing practices leaves much to be desired among the majority of women surveyed. The beliefs they hold about foods to be chosen and to be avoided during pregnancy and lactation have no scientific basis. These beliefs have taken root by tradition, culture and time.

9. Since women can play a significant role in shaping the nutritional patterns of families the following recommendations are made based on the findings of the present survey.

Better educational facilities should be provided to all the women and specially to the Muslim women who are deprived of even the minimum education.

Work opportunities and facilities outside the home should be created for all women such that their family income status can be improved. The women among the backward groups need to be encouraged to the advantage of take opportunities created.

Since nutrition and health knowledge and child care practice are generally poor among the women of different religious groups special education programmes need to be developed and offered to women organised into groups such as the Mahila Mandals.

To be able to develop leadership qualities and to play their role better in the development of their families, women need to be organised into small groups for discussion and interaction on matters of common interest to them.

These women's groups should be the nerve centres for all development programmes related to women and children.

References

1. A Review of Nutrition Studies in India in *"Diet Atlas of India"*—I.C.M.R., New Delhi, 1951.

2. Arora, D.D. and Kaul, K.K.—*Feeding Practices During the First Five Years Among Central Indian Communities,* Ind. J. Paediatrics, Vol. 40, pp. 203, 1973.

3. Austin, J.E. and Levinson, F.J.—*Family Planning Resume, 'Population and Nutrition;—A Case for Integration',* Sec. D., Vol. 1, pp. 241, 1977, Community and Family study Centre, University of Chicago.

4. Aykroyed, W.R.—*"Nutrition Newsletter",* J. Home Economics, Vol. 53, 1968.

5. Aykroyed, W.R.—*"Reflections on Human Food Patterns",* Nutr. pp. 65-70, 1961.

6. Bageli, K., Subal Roy and Nibha Sengupta—*"The Impact of Urbanisation on Dietary Habits and on Nutritional Status",* J. Ind. Dietet. Assn., Vol. 2, pp. 20, 1964.

7. Basel, S.K.—*"Nutrition Education"* in World Reviews of Nutrition and Dietetics, 5: 14, 1965.

8. Bender, A.E.—*Nutritional Status of School Children,* Symposium on *'Social and Economic Factors in Human*

Nutrition', Proc. Nutr. Soc. 33:45: 1974, Cambridge University Press.

9. Brown, I.C.— *Understanding Other Cultures.* Prentice-Hall, Eagle Wood Cliffs, N.J., 1955.

10. Burgess, A. and Dean, R.F.A.—*"Food Supplies and Consumption"* in *Malnutrition and Food Habits,* Chap. 2, pp. 9 Tavistock Publications, 1962.

11. Burgess, A. And Dean, R.F.A—*"The Social Psychology of Food Habits"* in *Malnutrition and Food Habits,* Chap. 6, pp. 81, Tavistock Publications, 1962.

12. Byrne, M.S.R.N., Cert and H.V. Tutor Cert.—*"Nutrition Education in the Home",* The J. Trop. Paediatrics and American Child Health, Vol. 8, No. 1, pp. 22, 1962.

13. Cassel, J.—*"Social and Cultural Implications of Food and Food Habits",* Am. J. Pub. Health, 47, 732, 1957.

14. *Census of India—Age Tubules Paper No. 2,* Office of the Registrar General of India, Ministry of Home Affairs, New Delhi, 1969.

15. Copping, A.M.—*"Planning Nutrition Education in Developing Countries",* J. Am. Dietet. Assn., 53: 127: 1968.

16. Degarine, I.—*"Rapport Surles Habitudes Alimenteries an dans la Region Dikhombole",* Rome R.A.O (Mimeo), 1960.

17. Devadas, T.P.—*Social and Cultural Factors Influencing Malnutrition,* Proc. Nutr. Soc. Ind., No. 6, 1968.

18. Devadas, R.P.—*Social and Economic Dimensions of Nutrition,* Proc. Nutr. Soc. Ind. No.17, 1974.

19. Devadas, R.P., Eswaran, P.P.—*"Influence of Socio-economic Factors on the Nutritional Status and Food Intake of Pre-school Children in a Rural Community",* J. Nutr. and Dietet., Vol. 4, pp. 156, 1967.

20. Dhillan, H.S., J.R. Yadhav.—*"Dietary Habits and Beliefs During Pregnancy and Lactation in Rural Bengal",* Cyclostyled Paper.

21. Divekar, S.—*"A Study of Child Rearing Practices Among Marathi Middle Class"*, S.N.D.T. University, Bombay, (Unpublished thesis), 1967.

22. Edwards, C.E., H. Moswain and S. Haire—*"Odd Dietary Practices of Women"*, J. Am. Diet. Assn., 30:976, 1954.

23. Edward Wellin.—*Cultural Factors in Nutrition, Nutrition Reviews*, Vol. 13, pp. 129-131, 1955.

24. Eppright, E.S.—*"Factors Influencing Food Acceptance"*, J. Am. Diet. Assn., 23: 579, 1947.

25. *Family Expenditure Survey Report for 1969*, H.M.S.O., London, Nutr. Ab. and Reviews, 41, 1308, 1971.

26. Fathaver, G.H.—*"Food Habits—An Anthropologists Views"*, J. Am. Diet. Assn., 37: 335, 1960.

27. Fleck, H. and E. Munves—*"Food Habits"*, in Introduction to Nutrition, Chap. 1 and 3, pp. 1 and 34, New York, The Macmillan Company, 1962.

28. Florencio, C.A.—*"The Efficiency of Food Expenditure Among Certain Working Class Families in Columbia"*, Nutr. Ab. and Reviews, 39, 1969.

29. Foll, C.V.—*"An Account of Some of the Beliefs and Superstitions about Pregnancy, Parturition and Infant Health in Burma"*, The J. Trop. Paediat. Vol. 5, No. 2, pp. 51, 1959.

30. Foster, G.M.—*"Cultural Barriers to Change", in Traditional Cultures and the Impact of Technological Change"* Chap 5, pp. 76-77, Harper and Rav Publishers, New York and Evanston, 1962.

31. Ghosh, B.N.—*Feeding Habits of Infants and Children in South India (on 600 families)*, Ind. J. Med. Res., Vol. 54, pp. 88, 1966.

32. Ghosh, S., Gidwani, S., Mittal, S.R. Verma, R.K.—*"Socio-Cultural Factors Affecting Breast Feeding and Other Infant Feeding Practices in an Urban Community*. Indian Paediatrics, Vol. XIII, pp. 26, 1976.

33. Gopalan, C.—*Major Nutritional Problems of India and South East Asia Proc. Seventh International Congress of Nutrition,* Humburg, III. pp. 320, 1966.

34. Gopalan, C.—*"Nutrition Fertility and Reproduction"*, Proc. Nutr. Soc. India, NIN, No.14, pp. 49, 1973.

35. Gopalan, C.—*Nutritional Status of India's Children,* N.F.I. Bulletin, Vol. 7, No.1, 1986.

36. Guthe, C.E., and Mead, M. *"Manual for the Study of Food Habits",* Bulletin of the Nat. Res. Cann. No. 111, Nat. Acad. Sci., Washington, D.C. 1943.

37. Harlog, D.C—*"Culture and Nutritional Advice in the Netherlands"* cited from Malnutrition and Food Habits by Burgess and Dean, 1962.

38. Hausen, G.R.—*"An Index of Food Quality",* Nutr. Reviews, 31:1, 1973.

39. *Health Statistics of India (1950).*—Et. Sci. Ministry of Health, Govt. of India, New Delhi, 1950.

40. Hilary Land—*Poverty and Welfare Policies,* Symposium on *'Social and Economic Factors in Human Nutrition',* Proc. Nutr. Soc. 33; 39: 1974, Cambridge University Press.

41. Igor De Garine—*The Socio-cultural Aspects of Nutrition, Ecology of Food and Nutrition,* Vol. 1, pp. 143, 1972.

42. Indira Bai, K.—*"Role of Cultural Beliefs in Infant Nutrition with Reference to Population Education",* 1974 (unpublished).

43. Inana, M. D.T. Pringle and Louse Little—*"Dietary Survey of Low Income Rural Families in Iowa and North Caroline",* J. Am. Diatet. Assn. 66; 356, 1944.

44. Jaiswal, O.P., Malik, A., Ansari, Z., Sinha, S.N.—*'Study of Feeding Practices and Morbidity Pattern During First Year of Life',* Ind. Paediatrics, Vol. 8, pp. 735 1981.

45. Jalso, S.B., Burns, M.M.—Rivers, J.M.—*Nutritional Beliefs and Practices,* J. Am. Diet. Assn. Vol. 47, pp. 263, 1965.

46. Jeen, P.L., M.B. Smith and G. Stearms—*"Dietary Habits of Pregnant Women of Low Income in Rural State"* J. Am. Dietet. Assn., 28; 27, 1950.

47. Jenner, A.—*"Social Emotional and Cultural Influences as Related to Eating Patterns and Malnutrition"*, Canadian Nutrition Notes, Vol. 24, No. 4, pp. 37-42, 1968.

48. Jelliffe, D.B.—*"Culture, Social Change and Infant Feeding in Tropical Region"*, J. Am. Cli. Nutr. 10:19, 1962.

49. Jhonston, B.F. and J.W. Mellon—*"The Nature of Agricultures Contribution to Economic Development"* Stanfer Food Research Institute Studies 1 (3), 335, 1960.

50. Joachin Kreysler and Irmgard Schulze Western—*Social Factors Influencing Attitudes of Mothers Towards Nutrition Services in Rural Population,* Ecology of Food and Nutrition, Vol. 2, pp. 49, 1973.

51. Judit Katoma—Apte—*The Socio-cultural Aspects of Food Avoidance in a Low Income Population in Tamilnadu, South India,* J. Trop and Paediatric and Environmental Child Health, Vol. 23, pp. 83 to 90, 1977.

52. Kumar, V., Sharma, S., Kanna, P., and Vanaja, K.,—*"Breast Vs Bottle Feeding—Impact on Growth in Urban Infant"* Ind. J. Paediatrics, 49: 271, 1981.

53. Lee, D.—*"Cultural Factors in Dietary Choice"*, Am. J. Clin. Nutr. 5, 116, 1957.

54. Leverton, R.M.—*"Food Fads"* in *Food Becomes You*, Chap 15, pp. 157, 2nd edition, Iowa State University Press, Ames. Iowa, 1960.

55. Lewin, K.—*"Factors Behind Food Habits and Methods of Change"*, Nat. Res. Coun. Bull. No. 108, Nat. Acad. Sci., Washington, D.C., pp. 36-37, 1942.

56. Lowenberg, M.E., Todhunter, E.N., Wilson, E.D., Surage, J.R. and Ludanski, J.C. (1974)—*Food and Man, 'Food, Man and Religion',* Chap. 5, pp. 125, Wiley Eastern Private Limited, New York.

57. Luggi, F.G.—*"Food Pattern and Nutrition in Religion French Polynesia"*, A. Co. No. 2, 298, 1962.

58. Magnus Pyke—*Food and Society 'Religion, Science and Nutrition'*, Chap. V. pp. 54, John Murray, Fifty Albermarle Street, London, 1968.

59. Maliha Parveen Khaman and Padma Umapathi—*"A Survey of Food Habits and Beliefs of Pregnant and Lactating Mothers in Mysore City"*, The Ind. J. Nutr. Dietet. 13:208, 1976.

60. Mathur, Y.C.—*Feeding Habits and Beliefs of Practical Significance in Villages: Impact of Urbanisation on Feeding Habits and Beliefs,* Ind. Paediatrics, Vol. 12, pp. 69, 1975.

61. Martin, E.A.—*"Your Food Habits and What They Mean"*, in Nutrition in Action; Chap. 1: pp. 3, 2nd ed. Holl, Rinchart and Winston, New York—Chicago—San Francisco—Toronto, London, 1965.

62. Martin, E.A.—*Roberts Nutrition Work with Children, Chicago.* The University of Chicago Press (1963), pp 19-20, cited from Devadas R.P.—*Social and Cultural Factors Influencing Malnutrition,* Proc. Nutr. Soc. Ind. No.6, pp. 6, 1968.

63. McKenzie—*The Impact of Economic and Social Status on Food Choices, Symposium on 'Social and Economic Factors in Human Nutrition,* Proc. Nutr. Soc.. Vol. 33, pp. 70-71, 1974, Cambridge University Press.

64. Mead, M.—*"Cultural Patterns and Technical Change" World Federation for Mental Health"*, Tensions and Tech. Scr., No.8 Paris, France, UNESCO, 1953.

65. Mehata, M.J. Pawn, R.G. and Betkenur, U.N.—*"Infant Feeding Habits in Surat City (South Gujarat)"*, Indian Paediatrics, Vol. 9, pp. 290, 1972.

66. Moller, M.S.G.—*"Customs, Pregnancy and Child Rearing in Tanganyika"* The Journal of Tropical Paediatrics and African Child Health, Vol. 7, No.2, pp. 66, 1961.

67. Montagn, M.F.A.—*"Nature, Nurture and Nutrition"*, Am. J. Clin. Nutr., 5: 237, 1957.

68. Moore, H.B.—*"Psychological Facts and Dietary Fancies"*, J. Am. Dietet Assn., 28: 759, 1952.

69. N.R.C.—*Nutritional Academy of Sciences,—National Research Council Bulletin No. 108, 1943,* cited from Devadas, R.P.—*Social and Cultural Factors Influencing Malnutrition,* Proc. Nutr. Soc. Ind. No.6, pp. 6, 1968.

70. *Nutrition and Fertility Inter-relationships Implications For Policy and Action*—National Academy of Sciences, Washington D.C., pp. 10, 1975.

71. Naik, J.P. and Kalpana Bardhan—*"Nutritional Problems of Women in India", Some Socio-economic Aspects,* Proc. Nutr. Soc. India, NIN, No. 17, 1974.

72. Ozala, E.M., Phil. D.—*"Consumption Patterns and Economic Progress"*, Chap. VII, pp. 87, *Agriculture and Economic Progress,* Oxford University Press, London, 1962.

73. Orr, J.—Proc. Nutr. Soc., 1: 7, 1945, cited from Usha J.M. and Devadas, R.P.—*"Diet Surveys",* Ind. J. Nutr. and Dietet, 1: 822, 1964.

74. Parvathi Rao, K.—*"Social Cultural Factors and Malnutrition in Telangana Region of Andhra Pradesh"*, Proc. Nutr. Soc. of India, No. 6 pp. 37, 1968.

75. Pekkariman, M.—*"World Food Consumption Patterns"*, Introduction *"Man, Food and Nutrition"*, pp. 16, Edited by Reclugle M, CRC Press, Cleveland, Ohio, 1973.

76. Phillips, D.E., Mary Ann Bass and Elizabeth Yetley—*Use of Food and Nutrition Knowledge by Mothers of Pre-school Children,* J. Nutr. Edu., Vol. 10, pp. 73, 1978.

77. Poleman, T.T., Perera, L.N., Fernando, W.I.M. and Beartric, V.D.—*"The Effect of Income and Food Habits in Sri Lanka"*, Nutrition Newsletter, FAO II, 9, 1973.

78. Prasada Rao, D.C.V.—*A Study of Social Aspects of Child Health in the Slum Communities of Pondicherry,* Ind. J. Paediatrics, Vol. 39, pp. 311, 1972.

79. Proudfit, F.T. and C.H. Robinson—*"Factors Influencing Food Habits and Their Modification"* in *Normal and the Therapeutic Nutrition,* Chap. 15, pp. 199, 12th ed. (1st Indian ed.), Pub. Oxford and I.B.M. Publishing Com. 36, Chowringhee Road, Calcutta, 16, 1965.

80. Prugh, D.E.—*"Psychologic Consideration with Problems of Over Nutrition",* The Am. J. Clin. Nutr., p. 9: 1961.

81. Puri, R.K., Khanna, K.K.,—*"Infant Feeding and Child Rearing Methods in Pondicherry",* Vol. 43, pp. 323, 1976

82. Ramathulasi, Y.—*A Study of Child Rearing Practices Among the Hindu Families in Tirupati",* S.V. University, Tirupati, May, 1969, (unpublished thesis).

83. Ranganathan, K.V.—*Some Thoughts on Nutrition Education,* Proc. Nutr. Soc. of India, No.6 pp. 1, 1968.

84. Rao, D.H. and S.C. Balasubramaniam—*Socio-cultural Aspects of Infant Feeding Practices in a Telangana Village",* Tro. Geographical Medicine, 18: 353, 1966.

85. Rao, K.V.—*Pattaern and Trends in Food Consumption in India,* Ind. J. Nutr. Diet. Vol. 14, pp. 79-87, 1967.

86. Rao, V.K.R.V.—*Purchasing Power as Determinant of Food Intake.* Proc. Nutr. Soc. India, Vol.23, pp. 13, 1978.

87. Reddy, P.R. and Peramma, D.—*Food Consumption Pattern Surveys Among Selected Communities of Chittoor District* Cited from *Food and Nutrition Monograph,* Ed. P.R. Reddy, S.V. University, Tirupati, Chap 13, pp. 41 to 61, 1977.

88. Ritchie, J.A.S.—*"Food Patterns and Nutrition in Teaching Better Nutrition"* Chap 1, pp. 4, F.A.O., Nutrition Studies, No.6 Washington, U.S.A, 1967.

89. Sai, F.T.—*Drastic Change in Food Habits in Relation to Socio-cultural Change, Pro. Seventh International Congress on Nutrition,* Humburg, III, pp 147-148, 1966.

90. Seers, R.P., Maccoby, E.E. and Levin, H.—*"Patterns of Child Rearing",* Row, Peterson and Co. New York, 1957.

91. Seth, V. Ghai, O.P.—*"Feeding Habits of Infants and Pre-school Children in Urban, Semi-urban and Rural Community",* Ind. Paediat., Vol. 8 pp. 452, 1971.

92. Shalini Bhogle—*"Child Rearing Practices Among Three Cultures"*, Social Change, Vol. 8, pp. 5-13, 1978.

93. Shirley, G. Langelaen—*The Impact of Economic and Social Status on Food Choice, Summary of Survey of Nutrient Intake of 234, 7th Grade School Children with Reference to School Milk,* Food and Nutrition Notes and Reviews, Vol. 32, pp. 12-15, 1975.

94. Shukla, R.S., Bhambul and Bhandan—*A Study of Superstitious Practices on Urban Five:* Indian Paediatrics, Vol. 15, pp. 403, 1979.

95. Shyamalamba, C.H. Nagaraj Rao, M., Rao, G.P.,—*Nutritional Status of School Children—A Comparative Study in Two Ethnic Groups in Hyderabad City.* Indian Paediatrics, Vol.13, pp. 635, 1976.

96. Sharma, P., C.M.S. Siddhu and Prasad, B.G.—*"Feeding Pattern and Nutritional Status of Children Under Five Years in an Urban Area"*, Indian Paediatrics, Vol. 9, No.5, pp. 532, 1972.

97. Sindhu, L.S., Grewal, R., Bhatnagar, D.P.A *A Study of Physical Growth in Breast Fed and Bottle-fed Male Infants"*, Ind. J. Paediatrics, Vol.48, pp 75-79, 1981.

98. Sohan, L. Manocha—*"Malnutrition and Food Habits" in Malnutrition and Retarded Human Development"*, pp. 208, Charles, Thomas Publications, U.S.A.

99. Sohan Lal Nagda.,—*Population Science—A Multidisciplinary Study, 'Role of Certain Aspects of Home Science,* in Population Education by Dept. of Home Science S.V. University, Population Studies Centre, S.V. University, Tirupati.

100. Spreading the *"Good Nutrition Gospel", Freedom from Hunger, Vol. 8,* No. 50. pp. 10, Magazine of the Food and Agriculture Organisation, 1967.

101. Swaminathan, M.—*Essentials of Food and Nutrition 'Food Faddism and Faulty Food Habits"*, Vol. II, pp. 341, Ganesh and Company, Madras, 1974.

102. Teulon, P.N.—*Nutrition News Letter,* J. of Home Economics, Vol. 6, pp. 53-55, 1968.

103. Thimmayamma, B.V.S Parvathi Rao, and Visweswara Rao, K.—*Socio-economic Status, Diet and Nutrients Adequacies of Different Population Groups in Urban and Rural Hyderabad,* Ind. J. Nutr. and Dietet, 19, 173, 1982.

104. Thimmayamma, Satyanarayana, Parvathi and Swaminathan—*"The Effect of Socio-economic Differences on the Dietary Intake of Urban Population in Hyderabad.* The Ind. J. Nutr. 'Dietet. Vol. 10, pp. 81, 1973.

105. Udani, P.M.—*Urbanisation and Malnutrition, Indian Paediatrics,* Vol. 12, pp. 69, 1975.

106. *United Nations Development Review,* No. 2, 1970.

107. Valassi, K.V.—*"Food Habits of Greek Americans",* The An. J. Clin. Nutr., pp. 240, 1962.

108. Vijaya Kumar, Shiela Tanaja, Manjeet Real, Madhu Nundu, Vanaja, K.—*Beliefs and Practices of Rural Mothers Regarding 'Hot' and 'Cold' Food During Childhood Illness,* Indian Paediatrics, Vol. 18, pp. 871, 1981.

109. Wadhwer, S.J., Wagle, C.S.—*"Feeding Pattern and Nutritional Status of Infants",* Paediatric Clinics of India, Vol. 9, pp. 119, 1974.

110. Williams, S.R.—*Nutrition and Diet Therapy, 'Cultural, Social and Psychological Influences on Food Habits',* Chap. 13, pp. 254, The C.V. Masby Company, Saint Lowis, 1973.

111. Wilson, D.C. and E.M. Widdoson—*'A Comparative Nutritional Survey of Various Indian Communities',* Ind. Med. Res. Memoris, No. 34, pp. 1-20, 1942.

112. Wilson, M.M. and M.W. Lamb—*"Food Beliefs as Related to Ecological Factors in Common",* J. Home Economics, 60:115, 1968.

113. Whiteman, J.—*"Food Habits in Nigeria",* Nutr., pp. 136-140, Autumn, 1961.

114. Yudkin, J. and McKenzie, J.C.—*Changing Food Habits, London,* Macgibbon and Kee, pp. 15-27, 1964.

Index